First World War
and Army of Occupation
War Diary
France, Belgium and Germany

59 DIVISION
176 Infantry Brigade
Royal Welsh Fusiliers
4th Garrison Battalion
1 May 1918 - 30 April 1919

WO95/3021/12

The Naval & Military Press Ltd
www.nmarchive.com
Published in association with The National Archives

Published by

The Naval & Military Press Ltd

Unit 10 Ridgewood Industrial Park,

Uckfield, East Sussex,

TN22 5QE England

Tel: +44 (0) 1825 749494

www.naval-military-press.com

www.nmarchive.com

This diary has been reprinted in facsimile from the original. Any imperfections are inevitably reproduced and the quality may fall short of modern type and cartographic standards.

© **Crown Copyright**
Images reproduced by permission of The National Archives, London, England, 2015.

Contents

Document type	Place/Title	Date From	Date To
Heading	WO95/3021/12		
Heading	59th Division 176th Infy Bde 26th Bn Roy Welsh Fusiliers 1918 May Apr 1919 (Formerly 4th Bn R.W.F)		
Heading	59th Division 176th Infy Bde 4th Bn Roy Welsh Fusiliers May-Jun 1918 (Became 26th Bn Jly 1918)		
Heading	War Diary of 4th Garr Battn. Royal Welsh Fus From May 1st 1918 To May 31st 1918 Vol 1		
War Diary	Lattre St Quentin	01/05/1918	18/05/1918
War Diary	Houvelin	19/05/1918	20/05/1918
War Diary	Fiefs	21/05/1918	21/05/1918
War Diary	Blessy	22/05/1918	22/05/1918
War Diary	Herbelle	22/05/1918	22/05/1918
War Diary	Inghem	23/05/1918	25/05/1918
War Diary	Mussent	26/05/1918	31/05/1918
Heading	War Diary 4th Garrison R.W.F Volume XXV June 1st June 30th 1918		
War Diary	Mussent	01/06/1918	16/06/1918
War Diary	Laires	16/06/1918	30/06/1918
Operation(al) Order(s)	Operation Order No.1 By Lieut-Colonel E.H. Thruston Commanding 4Th Garr Bn. Royal Weich Fusrs	00/05/1918	00/05/1918
Operation(al) Order(s)	Operation Order No.2 By Lieut-Colonel E.H. Thruston Commanding 4Th Garr Bn. Royal Weich Fusrs	19/05/1918	19/05/1918
Operation(al) Order(s)	Operation Order No.3 By Lieut-Colonel E.H. Thruston Commanding 4Th Garr Bn. Royal Weich Fusrs	20/05/1918	20/05/1918
Operation(al) Order(s)	Operation Order No.4 By Lieut-Colonel E.H. Thruston Commanding 4Th Garr Bn. Royal Weich Fusrs	21/05/1918	21/05/1918
Operation(al) Order(s)	Operation Order No.5 By Lieut-Colonel E.H. Thruston Commanding 4Th Garr Bn. Royal Weich Fusiliers	22/05/1918	22/05/1918
Miscellaneous	Brigade Defence Scheme "B.B" Line No.3	07/06/1918	07/06/1918
Miscellaneous	To All Recipients Of Battn Defence Scheme	15/06/1918	15/06/1918
Map	Battalion Defence Scheme No.3 Sub-Sector II Sector "B.B" Line		
Operation(al) Order(s)	Operation Order No.1 By Major R.S. Browning Commanding 4th Garr Bn. The Royal Welsh Fusiliers	15/06/1918	15/06/1918
Operation(al) Order(s)	Operation Order No.XXX By Major R.S. Browning Commanding 4th Garr. Bn. Royal Welsh Fusiliers	26/06/1918	26/06/1918
Miscellaneous	Scheme For Practice In Trench Routine	26/06/1918	26/06/1918
Heading	War Diary of 26 Bn Royal Welch Fusiliers From July 1st 1918 To July 31st 1918		
War Diary	Laires	01/07/1918	06/07/1918
War Diary	Marest	13/07/1918	23/07/1918
War Diary	Wailly	24/07/1918	25/07/1918
War Diary	Line Round Mercatel	25/07/1918	31/07/1918
Operation(al) Order(s)	Operation Order No.XXXII By Lieut-Colonel E.H. Thruston Commanding 4Th Garr Bn. Royal Welch Fusiliers	08/07/1918	08/07/1918
Operation(al) Order(s)	Operation Order No.XXXIII By Lieut-Colonel E.H. Thruston Commanding 4Th Garr Bn. Royal Welch Fusiliers	00/07/1918	00/07/1918

Type	Description	Start	End
Operation(al) Order(s)	Operation Order No.XXXIV By Lt. Colonel H.H. Lee D.S.O. Cmdg 26th Bn. The	23/07/1918	23/07/1918
Operation(al) Order(s)	Operation Order No.XXXV By Lieut Colonel H.H. Lee D.S.O. Commanding 26th Bn. Royal Welsh Fusiliers	25/07/1918	25/07/1918
Operation(al) Order(s)	Operation Order No.XXXVII By Lt Colonel H.H. Lee D.S.O.	30/07/1918	30/07/1918
Heading	War Diary 26th Bn Royal Welsh Fusiliers From August 1st 1918 To August 31st 1918		
War Diary	Line Near Mercatel	01/08/1918	03/08/1918
War Diary	Barly	03/08/1918	08/08/1918
War Diary	Line Near Mercatel	09/08/1918	14/08/1918
War Diary	Bretencourt	15/08/1918	20/08/1918
War Diary	Chat Maigre Support Near Mercatel	21/08/1918	23/08/1918
War Diary	Saulty	24/08/1918	24/08/1918
War Diary	St Hilaire-Cottes	25/08/1918	25/08/1918
War Diary	La Pierriere	26/08/1918	31/08/1918
Operation(al) Order(s)	Operation Order No.XXXIX By Lieut-Colonel H.H. Lee D.S.O. Commanding 26th Royal Welsh Fusiliers	07/08/1918	07/08/1918
Operation(al) Order(s)	Operation Order XL By Lieut-Colonel H.H. Lee D.S.O. Commanding 26th Royal Welsh Fusiliers	11/08/1918	11/08/1918
Operation(al) Order(s)	Operation Order XLII By Lieut-Colonel H.H. Lee D.S.O. Commanding 26th Royal Welsh Fusiliers	30/08/1918	30/08/1918
Operation(al) Order(s)	Operation Order XLIII By Lieut-Colonel H.H. Lee D.S.O. Commanding 26th Royal Welsh Fusiliers	26/08/1918	26/08/1918
Heading	War Diary 26th Ryl. Welsh Fus September-1918 Vol.XXVII		
War Diary	Asylum St Venant	01/09/1918	02/09/1918
War Diary	Q6C 32.98 Sheet 36 A	03/09/1918	04/09/1918
War Diary	Lestrem	05/09/1918	12/09/1918
War Diary	Picantin	13/09/1918	13/09/1918
War Diary	Pont Riqueul	14/09/1918	29/09/1918
War Diary	R.5 (Sheet 36 A)	30/09/1918	30/09/1918
Operation(al) Order(s)	Operation Order No. XLIV By Lieut-Colonel H.H. Lee D.S.O. Commanding 26th Royal Welsh Fusiliers	03/09/1918	03/09/1918
Miscellaneous	Recipients Of Tonight's Orders	02/09/1918	02/09/1918
Operation(al) Order(s)	Operation Order XLIX By Lieut-Colonel H.H. Lee D.S.O. Commanding 26th Royal Welsh Fusiliers	28/09/1918	28/09/1918
Heading	War Diary 26th R.W.F. October 1st-31st 1918 Volume XXVIII		
War Diary	R5 (Sheet 36 A)	01/10/1918	02/10/1918
War Diary	Bac St Maur	03/10/1918	03/10/1918
War Diary	La Vessee Post	04/10/1918	05/10/1918
War Diary	Pear Tree Farm	05/10/1918	06/10/1918
War Diary	L'armee Post	07/10/1918	10/10/1918
War Diary	Ferme De Buez	11/10/1918	16/10/1918
War Diary	Marquette	17/10/1918	17/10/1918
War Diary	Recuil	18/10/1918	18/10/1918
War Diary	Sailly-Lez Lannoy	19/10/1918	20/10/1918
War Diary	Holans	21/10/1918	22/10/1918
War Diary	Toufflers	23/10/1918	02/11/1918
Heading	War Diary 26th Battalion Royal Welch Fus Volume XXX November 1918		
War Diary	Toufflers	01/11/1918	08/11/1918
War Diary	Chaos	09/11/1918	09/11/1918
War Diary	Grand Rejet	10/11/1918	10/11/1918

War Diary	Delpre	11/11/1918	12/11/1918
War Diary	Grand Rejet	13/11/1918	14/11/1918
War Diary	Moorcourt	15/11/1918	15/11/1918
War Diary	Templeuve	16/11/1918	16/11/1918
War Diary	Thumesnil	17/11/1918	30/11/1918
Heading	War Diary December 1918 Volume XXXI 26th Batt. Royal Welsh Fus.		
War Diary	Thumesnil	01/12/1918	06/12/1918
War Diary	Barlin	07/12/1918	31/12/1918
Heading	War Diary January 1919 Volume XXXII 26th Batt. Royal Welsh Fus.		
War Diary	Hondeghem	01/01/1919	17/01/1919
War Diary	Hondeghem Stagine Camp	18/01/1919	29/01/1919
War Diary	Dunkirk	30/01/1919	31/01/1919
Heading	War Diary February 1919 Volume XXXIII 26th Batt. Royal Welsh Fus		
War Diary	Dunkirk	01/02/1919	28/02/1919
Heading	War Diary March 1919 Volume XXXIV 26th Batt. Royal Welsh Fus		
War Diary	Dunkirk	01/03/1919	20/03/1919
War Diary	Malo-Les-Bains	21/03/1919	31/03/1919
Heading	War Diary April 1919 Volume XXXV 26th R.W. Fus.		
War Diary	Malo	01/04/1919	30/04/1919

W95/3021/12

59TH DIVISION
176TH INFY BDE

26TH BN ROY. WELCH FUSILIERS
1918 MAY – APR 1919

(FORMERLY 4TH BN R.W.F.)

To EGYPT 54 DIV 162 BDE

26th Bn. R.W. Fus

59TH DIVISION
176TH INFY BDE

4TH BN ROY. WELCH FUSILIERS
MAY - JUN 1918
(BECAME 26TH BN JLY 1918)

4th Garr. Battn. R. W. Fus.
1918

Army Form C. 2118.

WAR DIARY
or
INTELLIGENCE SUMMARY
(Erase heading not required.)

Original

War Diary

4th Garr. Bttn. Royal Welch Fus.

from May 1st 1918
to May 31st 1918

Confidential

Became 26 R.S.R. Regt
16.7.18

Army Form C. 2118.

WAR DIARY
or
INTELLIGENCE SUMMARY.
(Erase heading not required.)

Instructions regarding War Diaries and Intelligence Summaries are contained in F. S. Regs., Part II. and the Staff Manual respectively. Title pages will be prepared in manuscript.

Place	Date	Hour	Summary of Events and Information	Remarks and references to Appendices
Hulle s/c Quentin	1/5/18	—	Battalion furnished 5 officers & 300 men for R.E. work. Remainder - training in sector. Night operations in march. Weather wet.	R&JS
	2/5/18	—	Battalion furnished 4 officers & 300 men for R.E. work. Remainder - improving defences & training. Weather fine. Roads fair.	R&JS
	3/5/18	—	Battalion furnished 2 officers & 130 men for work under R.E. Remainder - improving defences & training. Weather fine. Roads very good	R&JS
	4/5/18	—	Battalion furnished 2 officers & 150 men for work under R.E. Remainder - improving defences & training. Weather very fine. Roads very good	R&JS
	5/5/18	.	Battalion rest - Weather wet to fair. Roads heavy.	R&JS
	6/5/18		Battalion at work on French sector all day. Weather fair - Roads good	R&JS
	7/5/18		Battalion at work on trenches all day. Weather very good - Roads good	R&JS
	8/5/18		Battalion inspected when at work on trenches by Lt. Gen. Sir W. E. Peyton K.C.B. KCVO DSO Corps Reserve Army. Weather very fine - Roads excellent.	R&JS
	9/5/18		Battalion at work on trenches all day - Weather fine - Roads good.	R&JS
	10/5/18		Battalion at work on trenches all day. Weather good - Roads good	R&JS
	11/5/18		Battalion engaged on work on trenches all day - Weather good. Roads good. 2/Lt J. Cragg 5 Yks Bn R.A.F. returned for [duty]	R&JS
	12/5/18		Battalion parade for divine service - No work - Weather fine - Roads good	R&JS
	13/5/18		Battalion at work on sector - Weather fine - Roads good	R&JS
	14/5/18		Battalion at work on sector. Weather fine. Roads good	R&JS
	15/5/18		Battalion at work on sector. Weather fine Roads good	R&JS
	16/5/18		Battalion at work on sector. Joined 176" Inf. Bgde 59" Divn. Weather fine. Roads good	FH&JH+
	17/5/18		Battalion at work on sector. Attempt to bomb village by enemy aeroplanes. Driven off by our aircraft & AA fire. Weather fine Roads good. Strength officers 25 other ranks 1030	FHB JHB

WAR DIARY
or
INTELLIGENCE SUMMARY.

(Erase heading not required.)

Army Form C. 2118.

Instructions regarding War Diaries and Intelligence Summaries are contained in F. S. Regs., Part II. and the Staff Manual respectively. Title pages will be prepared in manuscript.

Place	Date	Hour	Summary of Events and Information	Remarks and references to Appendices
Lillers	18/5/18	4pm	Battalion received orders to move to MAGNICOURT-EN-COMTE. Weather fine, roads good.	App/App.I
Quentin	19/5/18	11am	Battalion marched out of LATTRE ST QUENTIN as per APPENDIX I & proceeded via NOUVEL VION - IZEL-LES-HAMEAU - TINQUES - RHETERS to MAGNICOURT-EN-COMTE. Billeted at HOUVELIN. Weather fine - roads good.	JM3
HOUVELIN				
"	20/5/18	4-30am	Battalion marched out of HOUVELIN via MAGNICOURT-EN-COMTE at 4am & proceeded to FIEFS via LATHIEUYE - VALHUON - TANGRY. Billeted for the night. Weather fine. Roads good.	Appendix II
		12-55pm		
FIEFS	21/5/18	4-30am	Battalion marched out of FIEFS & proceeded to BLESSY via FEBVIN-PALFART - FLESHIN - NUHEM - ESTREE BLANCHE. Billet for the night - Weather fine. Roads good.	Appx III
		11-45am		
BLESSY	22/5/18	5-30am	Battalion marched out of BLESSY & proceeded to HERBELLE via MARTHES-LILLERS Road via THEROUANNE.	Appendix IV
		9-40am	Rested in billets.	
HERBELLE		6-30pm	Marched out of HERBELLE to INGHEM.	
INGHEM		7.15	Billeted A Coy a HQ - B, C, D Coy under canvas in village. Weather very fine. Roads good.	
	23/5/18		Battalion rested & carried out inspection of SBR & Rifles &c. The undermentioned officers joined for duty:- 2/Lt R. MACDOUGALL - A.E.K MORGAN - A. OLIVER - J.A.D GILLESPIE - C.F. GRANT - J.R.K. JACK - W. KELLY. Weather fine - roads good.	JM3
	24/5/18		Battalion resumed & improved their protection. Weather wet - Roads heavy - Strength officers 32 Other ranks 1145	JM3
INGHEM	25/5/18		Battalion carried out training under Coy & Specialist arrangements. Orders received from HQ 126th Infantry Bde to move to MUSSENT. Capt C BEVAN reported for duty. Weather fine - roads good.	JM3.
	26/5/18		Battalion marched out of INGHEM at 4pm & encamped at MUSSENT. Weather fine - roads good.	JM3.
MUSSENT	27/5/18		Battalion worked on "D" Sector "BB" line & carried out training & other parties annexed from HB for employment with the transport. Weather fine - radio good.	JM3.

Army Form C. 2118.

WAR DIARY
or
INTELLIGENCE SUMMARY.
(Erase heading not required.)

Instructions regarding War Diaries and Intelligence Summaries are contained in F. S. Regs., Part II. and the Staff Manual respectively. Title pages will be prepared in manuscript.

Place	Date	Hour	Summary of Events and Information	Remarks and references to Appendices
NUSSENT	28-5-18		Battalion worked on "D" Sector of "BB" line + carried out training. Lt A.S.PHILIPSON e 9 Other ranks annual from M.Gun school at CAMIERS - weather fine - Roads good.	0145.
	29/5/18		Battalion worked on "D" Sector of BB Line. carried out training. Weather fine. Roads good	0145.
	30/5/18		Battalion worked on "D" Sector of BB Line + carried out training. Weather fine. Roads good	0145.
	31/5/18		Battalion worked on "D" Sector of BB Line + carried out training. Weather fine - Roads good. Strength Officers 34 Other Ranks 935 Horses 18	TM 9.

Certified true copy.
M.J.Schitz Lieut
4 Garrison Trust.

ORIGINAL

CONFIDENTIAL YB 2

WAR DIARY
4 Garrison R.W.F.

XXX
Vol IV

July 1917 — Dec 1918

Army Form C. 2118.

WAR DIARY
or
INTELLIGENCE SUMMARY.

(Erase heading not required.)

Instructions regarding War Diaries and Intelligence Summaries are contained in F. S. Regs., Part II. and the Staff Manual respectively. Title pages will be prepared in manuscript.

Place	Date	Hour	Summary of Events and Information	Remarks and references to Appendices
Musson	1-6-18	-	Battalion worked on "I" Sector of "BB" Line. Weather fine. Capt. J H GRIMLEY proceeded on leave to England.	TBMS
"	2-6-18	-	Battalion worked on "I" Sector of "BB" Line. Weather fine.	TBMS
"	3-6-18	-	Battalion worked on "I" Sector of "BB" Line. Weather fine.	TBMS
"	4-6-18	-	Battalion worked on "I" Sector of "BB" Line. Weather fine.	TBMS
"	5-6-18	-	Battalion worked on "I" Sector of "BB" Line. Weather fine.	TBMS
"	6-6-18	-	Battalion worked on "I" Sector of "BB" Line. Weather fine.	TBMS
"	7-6-18	-	Battalion worked on "I" Sector of "BB" Line. Weather fine. Defence Scheme for No. 3 Subsector "II Sector", "BB" Line issued to Coys. and Officers concerned. Appendix "A".	TBMS Appendix "A"
"	8-6-18	-	Battalion worked on "II" Sector of "BB" Line. Weather fine. Capt. F.W.GRANT (F. (W.S) reported for duty.	TBMS

Army Form C. 2118.

WAR DIARY
or
INTELLIGENCE SUMMARY.

(Erase heading not required.)

Instructions regarding War Diaries and Intelligence Summaries are contained in F. S. Regs., Part II. and the Staff Manual respectively. Title pages will be prepared in manuscript.

Place	Date	Hour	Summary of Events and Information	Remarks and references to Appendices
NIBSANT	9.6.18	7:30am	Battalion marched from Blgs to Missant. Weather fine. Rain at night.	App. 5
"	10.6.18		Battalion worked on "I" Sector of "BB" line. Weather wet	App. 5
"	11.6.18		Battalion worked on "I" Sector "BB" line. Weather fine	App. 5
"	12.6.18		Battalion worked on "I" Sector "BB" Line. Weather fine. Capt. T.E.M. COCHRANE (2/5 W.B.) proceeded on leave. Lieut. F.R. COOPER'S leave extended to 22nd June. (Army W.O.)	App. 5
"	13.6.18		Battalion worked on "I" Sector of "BB" line. Weather fine	App. 5
"	14.6.18		Battalion proceeded with work on "I" Sector "BB" line. Weather fine. Lt.Colonel E.H. THURSTON resumed command of 1/25 Lnfs Bgde - Vice Bgdr General COPE proceeded on leave.	App. 5
"	15.6.18		Battalion proceeded with work on "I" Sector BB line. Training was also carried out. Weather fine. Major R.B. BROWNING assumed command of the Battalion vice Lt.Colonel E.H. THURSTON. Capt. W.I. BURNS assumed duties of 2nd in Command vice Major R.B. BROWNING. Lieut. S.O. LOWRY assumed command of "C" Coy vice Capt W.I. BURNS. Amended TRBUC scheme for No.3 Subsector "I" Sector "BB" line issued down to O.C's of Coys & Officers with majors. Appendix "B"	Appendix "B"

Army Form C. 2118.

WAR DIARY
or
INTELLIGENCE SUMMARY.
(Erase heading not required.)

Instructions regarding War Diaries and Intelligence Summaries are contained in F. S. Regs., Part II. and the Staff Manual respectively. Title pages will be prepared in manuscript.

Place	Date	Hour	Summary of Events and Information	Remarks and references to Appendices
MONSSANT	16.6.18	3:45am	176th Bde Order No 111 d/15/6/18 ordering move to LAIRES received.	
		5:15am	Battalion marched out en route for LAIRES. Operation Order No 21 (Appendix "C") issued herewith incl. dress route difficult to Brigade Route. Actual route:- THEROUANNE — ENGUINEGATTE — ERNY-ST-JULIEN — BOMY — GREUPPE	P.T.O APPENDIX "C"
LAIRES	"	4pm	Arrived LAIRES 4pm Weather Variable.	B.P.S.
	17.6.18		Battalion rested in billets. Lt. H. KIRKCONNEL.S have enlisted to 26-3-18 (Army W.O.) Capt. BEVAN evacuated sick to ENGLAND 6-6-18.	TCSB.
	18.6.18		Battalion commenced period of intensive training about two months. Parades on Reconstruction, Drill & Arms. Reorganization reconnaissance with CHP Nos M.G./4.1.26 (a) commenced. Warfare fire	TCSB.
	19.6.18		Battalion drafts "Gun.Con" in designation Army 59 TMB & A-25/20 1/18.6.18. Training 2 Route march - 5 hours. Weather wet & unsettled. Capt J.H. GRINDLEY returns from leave.	F.war.
	20.6.18		Capt J.H. GRINDLEY resumes duties of Battalion. Battalion rested for 6 hours. Capt W.F. BURNS preceded on special leave. Weather variable.	T.gas.
	21.6.18		Battalion formed for 6 Route. Weather variable. Capt H.J.E. ANSTRUTHER & Capt W.W. MITCHELL reported return from PONT-DE-METZ	Gas.
	22.5.18		Rifle Range Battalion carried out Musketry Practice at 1st Army Musketry Camp beyond BEAUMETZ-LES-AIRES Weather Good.	F.war.

WAR DIARY or INTELLIGENCE SUMMARY

Army Form C. 2118.

Place	Date	Hour	Summary of Events and Information	Remarks and references to Appendices
MARSEB.	23-6-18	8am	Lieut. C.A. STARK & three other ranks reported from Command. Eighty five other ranks reported from detachments at PONT-DE-METZ. Half battalion carried out musketry on 1st Army Musketry Camp ranges.	18/25
		5/m	2nd Lieut. J. CRAGG proceeded on Transport Course under Divisional Train.	18/25
	24-6-18		Capt F. MYERS QM (RC) proceeded to 40th Division as is strength. Battalion carried out musketry. Weather variable & wet.	18/25
	25-6-18		Battalion marched 5 mile Route march via CUHEM, executed tactical scheme. Weather good. Heavy ground. Battalion resumes "GARRISON" in Lozinghem. (TRO. 129) 25/6/18 Arty.)	18/25
	26.6.18		Battalion carried out 6 hours training by day & 12 hours by night. (Other ranks spent on lines) Weather good	18/25
	27-6-18	8am	Lt. C.A. STARK proceeded on conducting duties to [?] WIR 7th Other Ranks marched BI & BII.	Appendix II /25
		9am	Battalion carried out French musketry scheme (Operation Order XXX). Outbreak of P.U.O. causing much sickness in new draft from PONT-DE-METZ.	18/25
	28.6.18		2nd Lieuts. J.A.H. GILLESPIE & W. KELLY proceeded to X Corps Infantry School for instruction. Q.M. a/Hon Lieut. J.T. MAHONEY reported for duty. Weather Good.	18/25
	29.6.18		Battalion carried out 6 hours training on Elementary Coy. Tactics. Weather Good.	18/25
	30-6-18		Lieut Col. F.H. THURSTON resumed Command of the Battalion — vice Major BROWNING (who resumed 2nd in Command) vice Capt. W.I. BURNS.	18/25

S.H. Pincson
Lieut. Colonel.
Commanding 2nd Bn. R. Welch Fusiliers.

Appendix I

OPERATION ORDERS NO.1.
by
LIEUT-COLONEL E.H. THRUSTON, COMMANDING 4TH GARR.BN: ROYAL WELCH FUSRS.

1. MOVE. The Battalion and its first line Transport will move tomorrow 19:5:18 to MAGINCOURT-EN-COMTE via NOUVEL VION, IZEl-le-HAMMEAU, TINQUES, CHELERS.

2. DRESS. Dress:- 'Battle Order', Rifles and Bayonets, 50 rounds S.A.A. and waterproof sheet.
Packs and blankets will be carried in transport lorry which will carry 40 boxes S.A.A.

3. STARTING POINT. Starting Point will be the Cross Roads - J.23. centre.

4. ADVANCE GUARD. The advance guard will consist of half platoon of "A" Company, the Pioneer Section, 2 Signallers and 1 bicycle orderly under Lieut H.T.R.HENDIN and will pass the starting point at 3.15 a.m.

5. TIME & ORDER OF MARCH. Troops will pass the starting point at the following times :-

Batt.H.Q. and remainder of "A" Company - Capt. I.E.M.COCHRANE 3.30 a.

"B" Company	- Captain W.W. MITCHELL	3.35 a.m.
"C" Company	- Captain W.I. BURNS.	3.40 a.m.
"D" Company	- (less one platoon and M.G.Section) Captain T. MOORE.	3.45 a.m.
1st line transport	- Lieut. LONG.	3.50 a.m.

Companies will maintain intervals of 100 yards on the march.
In the event of an Air Attack, Column of Route will divide - 2 files on each side of the road, Halt! and Officers Commanding Companies will, at their discretion, open fire.

6. REAR GUARD. Rear Guard will consist of 1 platoon of "D" Company under 2/Lieut. A.R.BOWDEN, who will march 300 yards in rear of 1st line of transport.

7. BAGGAGE. All H.Q. and Coy. baggage, including Officers' Kits will be placed in wagons opposite the respective H.Q. and Company Billets by 8.30 p.m. tonight.

8. ADVANCE PARTY. An advance party composed of 8 cooks and 2 sanitary men under the R.Q.M.S. will proceed in the first lorry carrying equipment, with breakfast, tea and dinner rations, dixies and fuel to a selected spot between TINQUES and BERLES and will there meet a Brigade Staff Officer and will there prepare a breakfast for the troops arriving at 8.0 a.m.

8a. REAR PARTY. A rear party of 20 O.Rs. and batmen will remain behind under the Q.M. and follow with equipment in the last lorry.

9. LORRIES. Arrangements for lorries double journeys will be made by the Q.M.

10. AMMUNITION. The ammunition limbers will carry 100.000 rounds S.A.A., including 60,000 rounds in bandoliers and 40 boxes.

11. The Q.M. will arrange for each man to have a cup of tea and a biscuit ration before starting.

(sgd) J.T.Gmolly

Capt.& Adjt.
May 1918. 4th Garr.Bn: Royal Welch Fusiliers.

Appendix II

OPERATION ORDER NO.2.
by
LIEUT-COLONEL E.H.THURSTON, COMMANDING 4TH GARR.BN: ROYAL WELCH FUSRS.

1. MOVE.
The R.W.F. will move tomorrow to FIEFS via LA THUIELOIE – VAULUX – TANGRY.

2. STARTING POINT.
1 The following units will pass the Starting Point – Reference 4000 Sheet 36 D. – Fork Roads O.34.6.0. – as follows :-

Battn. H.Q. – 4.0 a.m.
"D" Company – 4.2 a.m.
"C" Company – 4.4 a.m.
"B" Company – 4.6 a.m.
"A" Company – 4.8 a.m.
Transport – 4.10 a.m.

3. ROAD.
The second class road from ROCOURT to LA THUIEIOIE is in good condition.

4. DRESS.
Dress and Equipment as on 19:5:18.

5. DETAIL
The same men who were with Q.M. today, as loading party, will do loading on this march.

All ranks marching, will have, under Company arrangements, a tea and biscuit breakfast before starting.

LIEUT BLEASDALE on bicycle, will report as billeting officer to Area Commandant at FIEFS at 9.30 a.m. tomorrow.

The 4 Coy. Q.M.Ss. and H.Q. and Coy. Cooks on 2 limbers, and mess cart and officers kits will pass starting point with transport and proceed direct, ignoring halts, to 1 mile this side of TANGRY and prepare a camp for mid-day halt at a place to be selected and which they will be informed before arrival.

This party will have iron ration for the day put in their limbers at the first halt and will also carry the Battn. dixies and fuel.

Os.C. Companies are responsible that every one on the strength of the Companys, if not otherwise detailed, will move with Battalion.

(Sgd) J H Gridley

Capt.& Adjt.
19th May 1918.   4/Garr.Bn. Royal Welch Fusiliers.

SECRET.   APPENDIX III

                    OPERATION ORDER NO.3
                              by
    LIEUT-COLONEL E.H.THRUSTON, COMMANDING 4TH GARR.BN: ROYAL WELCH FUSRS.

    Ref. Map Sheet h/4 1/100000

1.
MOVE.   The R.W.F. will march tomorrow the 21st inst. to BLESSY.

2.
ROUTE.   FEBVIN - PALFART - FIEFHIN - CUHEM - ESTREE - BLANCHE.

3.
STARTING   Cross roads ½ mile N.E. of S. in FIEFS.
  POINT.

4.
TIME.   4.30 a.m.

5.
ORDER OF   H.Qs. "A" Coy. - "B" Coy. - "D" Coy. - "C" Coy. & Transport.
  MARCH.

6.
BAGGAGE.   Including dixies in 3 limbers, will be ready for marching off at
           4 a.m.

7.
ADVANCE   Lt. Bleasdale will proceed with lorry and 2 guides to BLESSY.
PARTY.

8.
~~REXMMKXX~~ Reports to Battn. H.Qs. en route after 1st halt.
REPORTS.

                                              (Sgd). T.H.Grindby

                                                          Capt. & Adjt.

20:5:1918.   4th Garr. Bn: The Royal Welch Fusiliers.

Copy No. 10.

APPENDIX IV

OPERATION ORDER NO.4
by
LIEUT.COLONEL R.H. JERNSTON, COMMANDING 4TH GARR. BN: ROYAL WELCH FUSRS.

21st May, 1918.

1. MOVE.	The B.N. will march tomorrow the 22nd inst to HERBELLE.
2. ROUTE.	MALINES - HAME then W. via THEROUANNE.
3. STARTING POINT.	FORK ROADS AT HAM, ½ inch N. of BLESSY.
4. TIME.	5.30 a.m.
5. ORDER OF MARCH.	H.Qs. "C", "D", "B" & "A" Companies.
6. BAGGAGE.	1st line transport will be packed at 5 a.m.
7. BREAKFAST.	4 a.m. under Company arrangements.
8. LORRIES.	Under arrangements of Q.M.
9. REPORTS.	To Battn. H.Qs. on march after 5 a.m.

(Sgd) JH Grindley

Capt. & Adjt.
4th Garr. Bn. The Royal Welch Fusiliers.

Copy No. 1 Commanding Officer.
"   "   2 Major E.B. Browning.
"   "   3 O.C. "A" Company.
"   "   4 O.C. "B" Company.
"   "   5 O.C. "C" Company.
"   "   6 O.C. "D" Company.
"   "   7 Transport Officer.
"   "   8 R.S.M.
"   "   9 R.Q.M.S.
"   " 10 War Diary.
"   " 11 Spare Copy.

APPENDIX V.

Operation Order No. 5
by
LIEUT.COLONEL E.H.THRUSTON, COMMANDING 4TH GARR. BN: ROYAL WELCH FUSILIERS.

22:5:18.   Reference Sheet Sc. 1/100000

1.
MOVE.   R.W.F. will move today 22:5:18 into canvas at INGHEM 1½ miles
             by road from HERBELLE.

2.
STARTING   Cross roads W. of H. in HERBELLE.
POINT.

3.
TIME.   3.30 p.m.

4.
ORDER OF   H.Qs. "D" - MTN "C" - "B" - "A" Companies.
MARCH.
             On arrival each Company will pitch its own camp in site
             ordered.

5.
REPORTS.   After 6 p.m. to Camp H.Qs.

                                              (Sgd) J H Emelty.

                                                       Capt. & Adjt.
                                        4th Garr. Bn: The Royal Welch Fusiliers

     Copy No. 1 to "A" Company.
       "   " 2 to "B" Company.
       "   " 3 to "C" Company.
       "   " 4 to "D" Company.
       "   " 5 to M.O.
       "   " 6 to R.S.M.
       "   " 7 to R.Q.M.S.
       "   " 8 to T.O.

Brigade Defence Scheme "B.B." line.   Appendix "A"
Copy No. "A"

No. 3 Sub-Sector - Garrison:- 4th Garrison Bn: The Royal Welch Fusiliers.

limits of Secton - L.11. b 28 exclusive to F.29 b 28 inclusive.

Designation.	limits From To.	Company Detailed.	Sector limits description.	Battle H.Qs.	Battle H.Q. Position description.	Remarks.
Right Sector.	L11b28 L6a92	"C"	L11b28 is the bank of a stream L6a02 is where the trench cuts the MUSSENT - ECQUES Road.	L6d43	Is a small pit under a hedge on the cart track from the quarry in MUSSENT to the Bn. Camp.(Close to the quarry.	
Centre Sector.	L6a02 F29d44	"A"	F29d44 is the thirtieth fire bay counting West from the MUSSENT-HEUNING HEN Road, and just where the trench enters green corn. At this point the fourth tree to the right of a small stunted tree in "front" coincides with a distant windmill. In rear a telegraph standard coincides with the white chateau of IESPINCY.	L5b44	The N.W. corner of a dark green field lying across the MUSSENT - HEMFAUT road from the Battn. Camp. A very low hedge surrounds field.	
left Sector.	F29d44 F29b28	"D"	F29b28 is where trench cuts road.	F29c99	Battle H.W. is where the corn crop terminates in a promontory at a field of roots (turnip type) to the N.W. of a turnip heap, perhaps about 300 yards N.W. of the right of the Coy. sector.	
Reserve Coy.	Reserve trench system neighbourhood of L4b42.	"B"	Distributed along trench for safety but not sufficiently scattered to interfere with mobility.	L4b42	Battle H.Qs. lies where the trench has an uncut gap is at a point exactly in line with the last tree on the South	

-2-

Designation.	limits * From To.	Company detailed.	Section limits description.	Battle H.Qs.	Battle H.Q. position description.	Remarks.
					of a row of trees on the INGHEM-BlIQUES road and the tall poplar at MUSSENT Farm.	

* "From" reference is exclusive, "To" reference is inclusive.

2. Stragglers Post will be at:-

Designation.	Company finding.	Approx. Map Reference.	Description.	Remarks.
S.P. 1.	"C"	L6c26.	Any suitable spot in vicinity may be chosen.	
S.P. 2.	"C"	L6a50	At road junction.	
S.P. 3.	"A"	F30c03.	Cross roads.	

NOTE. These posts will consist of 1 Officer, 1 Sgt. 12 other ranks.
DUTY:- Collect stragglers and place in main line of resistance to fill up intervals between posts.

3. Until rear lines have been constructed Companies will dispose troops on line of R.

4. The main line of resistance will be held at all costs.

5. Battle Stations will be manned on command "Man battle Stations" and Companies must be in position within three hours. They will select their own route and will move into trenches as if on ordinary reliefs. Care must be taken now to damage crops.

6. Battn. Transport will proceed to vicinity of BIENTQUES and report to Capt. R.McErlich, Q.M. 23rd Garr.Bn. lancs. Fusrs.

7. LEWIS GUNS:- Guns will be allotted as under:-

"C" Company.	"A" Company.	"D" Company.	A.A.Defence at Bat. Battle H.Qs.
4	2	2	1

On "Alarm" all lewis Gunners will report to 1G.O. at H.Q.Coy. Billet. The 1.G.O.will despatch teams and guns to report to O.C.Companies. Guns will be under O.C.Companies - 1.G.O. will be with Battn. H.Qs.

8. Signalling Sergt. will detail four runners to report to Brigade H.Qs. and will despatch signallers to the signalling stations at each Coy. and Battle H.Qs. O.C.Companies will detail two runners each to report to Battalion H.Qs.

9. All prisoners will be despatched to Batt. Battle H.Qs., escort 10%.

10. R.A.P. will be at L4d89 M.O. and staff will remain in Camp until further orders.

11. Box respirators will be worn at "alert" when in Battle Stations. Alarm signals should be improvised.

Box respirators will be put on in case of Gas bombardment, and alarms sounded and warning passed to Battn. H.Qs. and flank Battns.

12. Quartermaster and Staff and C.Q.M.Ss. will remain in billets until ordered out.

13. Companies will report:- (1) when in position. (2) when in touch with flanks. (3) any other information by visual signal service or by runners.

14. Batt. Battle H.Qs. is at L4b91.

15. Brigade Battle H.Qs. is at L10a26 sunken road.

16. Reference maps 36A, 36D, 1/40000.

Field.

2/lieut. A/Adjutant,

4th Garrison Bn: The Royal Welch Fusiliers.

Copy No. 1 to C.O.
Copy No. 2 to Major R.B.Browning.
Copy No. 3 to Transport Officer.
Copy No. 4 to Quartermaster.
Copy No. 5 to Lewis Gun Officer.
Copy No. 6 to Adjutant.
Copy No. 7 to Medical Officer.
Copy No. 8 to "A" Coy.
Copy No. 9 to "B" Coy.
Copy No.10 to "C" Coy.
Copy No.11 to "D" Coy.
Copy No.12 File.

To all recipients of Battn. Defence Scheme.

Appendix "B"

Adderdum 1 to 4th Garr. Bn. R.W.F. Defence Scheme for No. 3 sub-sector, "D" Sector, "B.B." line.

1. <u>limits of Sector</u>:- for L11b28 ------ F29b28, read:- L11b28 exclusive to F18a12 inclusive.

   <u>Right Sector</u>:- for L11b28 ------- L6a02 read:- L11b28 exclusive to F29d44 inclusive.

   Batt. H.Qs. - for L5d48 read L5b44
   Cancel descriptions.

   <u>Centre Sector</u>:- for L6a02 ------- F29d44 read:- F29d44 exclusive to F23b60 inclusive.

   Batt. H.Qs. - for L5b44 read:- cross roads at F22d84
   Cancel descriptions.

   <u>left sector</u>:- - for F29d44 ------- F29b28 read:- F23b60 exclusive to F18a12 inclusive.

   Batt. H.Qs. - for F29c94 read:- Road fork at F17c92.
   Cancel descriptions.

   <u>Reserve Coy</u>:-. - for location at L4b42 read F28 central.

   Batt. H.Qs. - for L4b42 read:- F28 central.
   Cancel descriptions.

2. <u>Stragglers Posts</u>:- Please add:-

   S.P. 4 "D" Coy.   F24a07.
   S.P. 5 "D" Coy.   F18a62.

6. For:- "Battn. Transport will proceed to etc." - read:- "Battn. Transport will proceed to E30d13 (sheet 36D) and report to Capt. Ballantine, 23rd Garr.Bn. Lancs. Fusrs.

7. <u>Lewis Guns</u>.
   For "C" Coy.. 4 guns - Battn. H.Qs. - 1 gun, road:- "C" Coy. - 2 guns, Battn. H.Qs. 3 guns.

10. R.A.P. For L4d89 - read:- - L5c22.

14. For Battalion Batt. H.Qs. L4b91 - read:- L5c24.

    Appendix 1 should be amended under 7 (above)

    Appendix 11 will be ~~employed~~ replayed shortly.

15:6:18.

2/lt. A/Adjutant,
4th Garr. Bn. The Royal Welch Fusiliers.

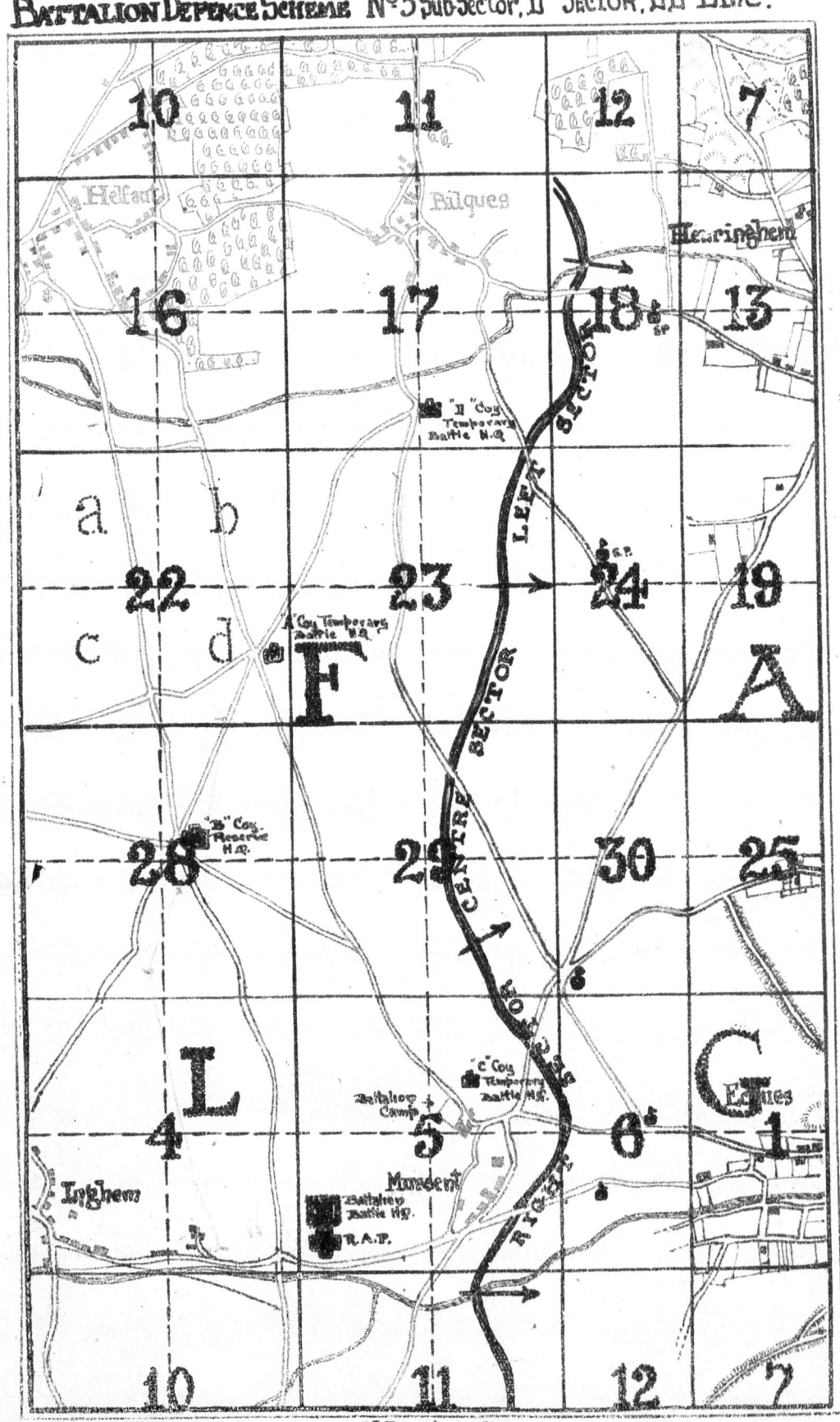

APPENDIX "C"

OPERATION ORDER NO.1.
by Major R.B.Browning
Commanding 4th Garr.Bn: The Royal Welch Fusiliers.

No. ....

16th June 1918.

1. MOVE. The Battalion will move tomorrow to LAIRES.

2. ROUTE. Route by les FAUBOURGS — THEROUANNE — ENGUINEGATTE — ERNY-ST-JULIEN — BOIS-DES-MAMES — LAIRES.
Mid-day halt at R.28.b. (Sheet 36D).

3. ADVANCE, REAR & BAGGAGE GUARD.
Advance Guard — One Platoon of "A" Company under 2/Lt. Oliver.
Rear Guard — One Platoon of "C" Company under 2/Lt. Morgan.
Baggage Guard — All P.l.D. men under 2/Lt. A.R.Bowden.

4. STARTING POINT. Starting Point at Cross Roads 1.5.b.6.1. (Sheet 36D) (Charing Cross).
Head of Column will pass Starting Point at 6 a.m.
Column in following order:— Advance Guard, Signallers, "A" Company, "B" Company, "C" Company, "D" Company, Lewis Gun H.Q. First line Transport - Rear Guard.

5. BAGGAGE. Baggage Commander will ~~report~~ remain behind and report to Quartermaster.

Lieut. A/Adjutant.
4th Garrison Bn: The Royal Welch Fusiliers.

OPERATION ORDERS NO. XXX
by
Major R.E. Browning,
Commanding 4th Garr. Bn. Royal Welch Fusiliers.

Reference Sheet 36D.

1. Battalion will take over trench sector X4.b32 – X5.d09 by midday 27.6.18.

2. "D" Coy. will take over subsector from X4.b32 to X5.a32.
   "C" Coy.   "   "   "   "   "   X5.a32 to X5.d09
   and report in position by 12 noon.

3. Composite Companies, under Lt. Mercer, (A. & B. Details) in reserve line at X10.b33, and will report in position by 12 noon.

4. Bn H.Q. will be at X10.b33.

5. Left flank held by X Batt. Sussex bears W.N.W. N.W. of BOAY.
   Right   "   "   " XX Liverpools   "   S.W. & S. of CUH...

6. Batt. S.A.A. Dump at X8.c11.

7.   "   Ration   "   " X4.b32.

8. Starting point Maires Church 9 a.m.

9. Order of march, Signallers, "D" & "C", Composite Coy.

10. Dress:- Battle order without helmets or respirator, with haversack rations and times.

Issued at 10 p.m.
26th June, 1918.

R.B. Webb Lt. for
Capt. & Adjt.
4th Garr. Bn. Royal Welch Fusiliers.

SCHEME for practice in TRENCH ROUTINE, 27th JUNE 1918.

INTRODUCTION.

The Battalion will practice Trench Routine and Reliefs tomorrow.

There is at present no trench system available and much will depend on the efforts of individual Officers and N.C.Os. to make a practice instructive under such conditions.

The Map, Sheet 36D, is exceedingly old and unreliable but it is the only material available in framing the scheme.

The present Map can be corrected by adding to the BOIS-de-MAMUS the farther area of wooded land enclosed by line X4.b.32 - X5.a.23 - X5.a.32 - X5.b.03 - X5.d.18 within this line to BOMY - CUHEM road, should be marked off as wooded ground.

GENERAL IDEA.

The Wood is open country but the paths through the wood are communication trenches. The Sector Front line is the line of the edge of the wood between X4.b.32 & X5.d.18. This must be imagined as a Trench divided at X5.a.22 into left and right Company Sectors. The front is ERNY-ST-JULIEN. The enemy's front line is the road R34.d.25 through R35.c.68 - X6.c.28.

SCHEME.

The Battalion will march out to X10.b.32 (where manoeuvre area begins) and 2 Companies will be detailed to man trenches. They will reconnoitre trenches moving by communication trenches (tracks and paths) X10.b.35. X5.d.18; X4.d.22 - X5.c.29 - X10.b.35 - X4.b.32. etc. and having laid down Front line and Support line and Communication Trench will lead Company in and take over from imaginary Battalion.

Range Cards will be made and saps, listening posts, wiring sites, M.G.posts and L.G.posts will be selected and all Routine gone through as laid down in Divisional Trench Orders.

Care must be taken to keep to a (path) communication trench once selected, troops must be kept interested and every endeavour made to make the practice instructive.

The two remaining Companies will in turn take over from the preceding ones and time that may be spent in waiting should be utilised in lectures and explanations to the men.

RECONNOITRING. Reconnoitring Officers will endeavour when selecting the trench lines at the beginning of the Scheme to make quick decisions. It must be borne in mind that the wood does not exist in the scheme and is only a means to allow of elasticity in selecting positions and to avoid damage

(over.

to crops were the practice carried out in open.

Zero hour at which Battalion marches past JAIRES Church as Starting Point will be 9.0 a.m.

Dress :- 'Battle Order' less helmet and respirator.

Order of March : Sig. D.C. [?] Coy.

T Buckley [?]
Capt. & Adjt.
26th June 1918.   4th Garr. Bn: Royal Welch Fusiliers.

CONFIDENTIAL.

WAR DIARY

of

26 Bn. ROYAL WELCH FUSILIERS

From July 1st 1918.
to July 31st 1918

WAR DIARY
INTELLIGENCE SUMMARY.
(Erase heading not required.)

Army Form C. 2118.

Instructions regarding War Diaries and Intelligence Summaries are contained in F. S. Regs., Part II. and the Staff Manual respectively. Title pages will be prepared in manuscript.

Place	Date	Hour	Summary of Events and Information	Remarks and references to Appendices
LAIRES	1-7-18		Battalion route marched to FIEFS. = 8 miles. Performed some training in afternoon. Weather fine	Pages.
"	2-7-18		Battalion carried out six hours training. Weather fine	Pages
"	3-7-18		Battalion bathed & carried out four hours training. Weather fine. Lieut. F.R. COOPER (on leave) ordered Medical Board by W.O. a shicks off. Strength Arthy. 176 Inf Bde. 566/3/1. Lieut. H. MARCONNEL (on leave) ordered Medical Board by W.O. a shicks off. strength Arthy. 176 Inf. Bde. 566/3/1.	Pages
"	4-7-18		Battalion bathed and carried out 2 to 6 hours training. Weather fine. Capt. H.J.E. ANSTRUTHER proceeded to 4th Army "A" for duty as Provost Reinforcement officer Arthy. AG. A/5ft 5398. 1st Army letter No. 1276/26822.	Pages.
"	5-7-18		Battalion carried out six hours training. Weather fine Captain J H GRINDLEY proceeded to Rifle Base classified unfit. — to "C" Infantry Base Depot Rouen. 2nd Lieut C.F. GRANT proceeded to Etaples - unfit - Arthy. AG A725/2 d/30/6/18 Lieut R.B. WEBSTER appointed Acting Adjutant vice Capt. J.H. GRINDLEY.	Pages.
"	6-7-18		Battalion practised trench manning and relief at R20 neighbourhood (Sheet 36 A) from 12am - 3pm. Weather fine.	Page 5

WAR DIARY
INTELLIGENCE SUMMARY
(Erase heading not required.)

Army Form C. 2118.

Instructions regarding War Diaries and Intelligence Summaries are contained in F. S. Regs., Part II. and the Staff Manual respectively. Title pages will be prepared in manuscript.

Place	Date	Hour	Summary of Events and Information	Remarks and references to Appendices
MARST	13-7-18		Battalion carried out Training & was inspected by G.O.C. III Army. Weather fine	App.1
"	14-7-18		Battalion rested. Weather variable	Pe 2r/s
"	15-7-18		Battalion carried out Route march via NEUVAL – ANTIGNEUL CHATEAU – BOURS. 8 miles. New training in afternoon.	Te 3rs
"	16-7-18		Battalion carried out 6 hours Training. Weather Fair.	Re 4/s
"	17-7-18		Battalion carried out simple Tactical exercises & training. Weather Fine.	Cn5
"	18-7-18		Battalion carried out 6 hours training – Weather fine. Lieut. ?. Shaw proceeded on leave.	Re 6/s
"	19-7-18		Battalion carried out Tactical Exercise in vicinity of PRESSY-LES-PERNES. Weather fine	Re 7
"	20-7-18		Battalion carried out Album Practice under Bgde Orders. Battalion ready to move 1 hour – 18 minutes. Battalion carried out 6 hours training & witnessed demonstration by H.A.C. Platoon. Weather fine	Re 8/s

Army Form C. 2118.

WAR DIARY
INTELLIGENCE SUMMARY.
(Erase heading not required.)

Instructions regarding War Diaries and Intelligence Summaries are contained in F. S. Regs., Part II. and the Staff Manual respectively. Title pages will be prepared in manuscript.

Place	Date	Hour	Summary of Events and Information	Remarks and references to Appendices
MARIEST	21-7-18		Sunday - Battalion rested. Brigade warned battalion to be ready to move forward. Lt. Col. H.H. LEE, Bokbn Offrs reported. 150 ORs	P&S
"	22-7-18	12am	Move cancelled by brigade. Battalion carried out training for OR Ranks. MAJOR R. REG. EYRE, Awaram Light Infty reported in duty.	P&S
"	23-7-18	4am	Bgde Order No 114 received. Lieut. Colonel E.H. THRUSTON - MAJOR R.E. BROWNING - Capt. W.E. BURNS - Lt. TWITTERUNNA proceeded to 59th Divisional Reception Camp SACHIN. Lt. Colonel H.H. LEE 150 assumed command of battalion.	Appx.
			Battalion inspected by R. of MAREST. 9 Buses at 9.15am and embussed at VALHUON & debussed at 5.30pm at BEAUMETZ-LES-LOGES & proceeded into billets at WAILLY. Weather very wet. Bgde Order No 115 received at midnight 23/24 July 1918.	Appendix ᄃ
WAILLY		6pm	CO, Coy Commanders & specialist officers reconnoitered subsector of 176th Bgde in order to ensure Divisional Front at MERCATEL with a view to taking over subsector on night 25/26th July 1918. Bgde Order No 116 received about 9.30 pm. Weather good.	
"	24-7-18	8am	Battalion Operation Order No XXV issued. Appendix. Battalion moved into left subsector in relief of 49th Canadian Battalion 7th Canadian Infty Bgde. Head of column reached trenches about 10.15pm. Relief reported complete at 2.16 am 25/7/18. The subsector boundary runs as follows: - Left Boundary M30a60 - M30a61 - M23d65,5 - M22d50 - M20c36. Right Boundary S6a15- M34c central	Appendix. ᄑ
HINE TUNNEL	25-7-18		Battalion in y/w. 26th Kings hverpool Regt. No casualties occurred during relief. Weather good.	
MERCATEL			Small Refs given above from France 51 B SW.]	

Army Form C. 2118.

WAR DIARY
INTELLIGENCE SUMMARY.
(Erase heading not required.)

Instructions regarding War Diaries and Intelligence Summaries are contained in F. S. Regs., Part II. and the Staff Manual respectively. Title pages will be prepared in manuscript.

Place	Date	Hour	Summary of Events and Information	Remarks and references to Appendices
In line round MERCATEL	26-7-18	2:35am	Hostile Blue Cross gas fell on right flank but concentration insufficient to cause casualties. Heavy French Mortar or High Explosive fire for few minutes between Observation line & Support line on Battalion extreme right front. No casualties. Day normal to quiet. Occasional isolated movement 目 behind enemy's lines. Weather - very wet from 2 hrs onwards. Casualties = one other rank wounded.	Appendix S.
"	27-7-18	5 am	Enemy Patrols reported Machine Guns at S.6.6.3.5 & a rifle post at S.6.6.2.0. Situation normal and visibility poor. Weather wet. Patrol at night established existence of hostile French Mortar at M.36.c.9.7. Casualties = Nil. Captain W.W. MITCHELL rejoined from leave but did not proceed beyond transport lines.	Appendix S.
"	28-7-18		Battalion conducted small inter-platoon relief in front line line, small patrols out during the day. Movement on enemy front below normal. Enemy shelled right flank support platoon and was quickly silenced by our artillery. Enemy aircraft very quiet. Weather fair. Casualties = one other rank wounded.	Appendix S.
"	29-7-18		Reconnaissance patrols out at night examining wire on right front & centre. Badly cut by T.M. fire. Visibility poor. Movement below normal. Weather fair. Casualties = nil observed. Much artillery activity on our right at night.	Appendix S.
"	30-7-18		Many patrols active for enemy artillery on our right. Movement normal. Evening quiet. Operation Order XXXIII issued to Coys & Officers concerned. Weather good.	Appendix H
"	31-7-18		Day moderately active as regards enemy artillery on right front. Details of Relief arranged. Much movement round battalion HQ during day, resulting in undoubtedly some intermittent shelling of right during relief. Battalion was relieved over sector by 3:30 am 1/8/18. & proceeded to "Brickfields". Very busy night arriving & after midnight. Casualties = 17.	Appendix S.

[signed] G 76 R W L Trotman

Map: Hazebrouck V2 Lens 11   **Appendix A**

OPERATION ORDER NO. XXXII
by
Lieut-Colonel E.H. THRUSTON
Commanding 4th Garrison Bn: Royal Welch Fusiliers.

1. MOVE — Battalion will march to EPS tomorrow the 9th instant.

2. ROUTE — PREDEVIN – HEUCHIN – BOYAVAL – EPS.

3. STARTING POINT — CROSS ROADS of LAIRES – PREDEVIN Road, and BEAUMETZ – FIEFS Road.

4. TIME. — 6.15 a.m.

5. ORDER OF MARCH. — H.Qrs., "D", "A", "B", "C" Companies.

Battalion Headquarters will close at 6.0 a.m.

Reports to B.H.Q. on march.

~~Reveille   – 4.30 a.m.~~
~~Breakfast – 4.45 a.m.~~
~~Parade   – 5.30 a.m.~~

Maps Hazebrouck V2. Lens 11.

                                                Lieutenant Actg. Adjutant.
8th July 1918.   4th Garrison Bn: The Royal Welch Fusiliers.

Appendix B
13.

OPERATION ORDER NO. XXXIII.
by
Lieut-Colonel E.H. HOUSTON
Commanding 4th Garrison Bn: Royal Welch Fusiliers.

Map Reference Sheet 44B.

1. MOVE. Battalion will march to MARMET and BOURS tomorrow the 16th instant.

2. ROUTE. HESTRUS – TANGRY – PRESSY-les-PERNES – or
HESTRUS – G35d99 – M8b98 – H28c79 – H28b92

3. STARTING POINT. Fork Roads – G33.a.7.2.

4. TIME. 7.15 a.m.

5. ORDER OF MARCH. Headquarters, "A", "B", "C" and "D" Companies.

Battalion Headquarters close at 6.30 a.m.

Reports to B.H.Q. on march.

Lieut.Acting Adjutant.
4th Garrison Bn: The Royal Welch Fusiliers.

July 1918.

Copy No. 1. 2/in Command.   Copy No. 10. Signalling Officer.
" 2 to 5. Os.C.Companies.   "   " 11. Lieut. Bradford.
" No. 6. M.O.   "   " 12. Captain Grant.
"   " 7. Q.M.   "   " 13. War Diary.
"   " 8. T.O.   "   " 14. War Diary.
"   " 9. I.S.O.   "   " 15. Spare.
                               "   " 16. R.S.M.

SECRET   Appendix C

OPERATION ORDER XXIV   Copy No ___

Map Ref   by
44B   Lt Colonel H.H. LEE DSO
           Cmdg 26th Bn The RWF

1. **MOVE**   The Battalion will march to VALHUON to embus

2. **STARTING POINT**
       Road junction H 28 b92

3. **HOUR**   9-15 am

4. **Order of MARCH**
       HQ, A, B, C, D Coys.

5. **DRESS**   Full marching order with one blanket per man. Blanket rolled round pack

6. **GENERAL**
       Coy Commanders will pay great attention to the cleanliness of their billets before marching off.

Issued 6.30 am   R.B.Sedgk Lt A/Adjt
Field   26th RWF
23-7-18

Distribution :— normal

OPERATION ORDER NO. ~~XXXIV~~ XXXV.
by
Lieut Colonel H.H. Lee D.S.O.
Commanding 26th Bn. Royal Welch Fusiliers.

1. The Battalion will relieve the 49th R. Canadian Regt. in the line tonight.
"A" Coy will relieve "A" Coy 49th R. Canadian Regt. in the line. Support
"B" " " " "B" " " " " " " " " "
"C" " " " "C" " " " " " " " Front line
"D" " " " "D" " " " " " " " " "

Each Platoon will relieve the similar numbered Platoon of the 49th Canadian Regt.
Each Company will take over the correct disposition of the 49th R. Canadian Regt.
Boundaries of Company in Front line are:-
"C" Coy. M30.a.8.0 - M36.a.4.7.
"D" " M36.a.4.7.- S6.a.1.5.

II. The Battalion will parade in Fighting Order, with Greatcoats rolled above haversack, at 6.30 p.m. ready to march off at 6.40 p.m.
Company Commanders will see that men's waterbottles are filled Respirators at 'Alert'.

III. Rations for the 26th will be cooked today and carried on the man.

IV. O.C.Companies will submit to Bn.H.Q. by 8a.m. 27/7/18, a list of all Maps, Aeroplane Photographs, Trench Stores, S.A.A.Grenades, Tools, R.E.Stores, Defence Schemes taken over.

V. All Packs and Kit not to be taken in to the trenches will be stacked by Platoons outside Huts by 3.0 p.m. today to be removed to the Transport lines. Blankets will be packed in Valises.
Officer's Kits will be stacked outside their respective Messes.

VI. Each man will take 2 pairs of socks into the line

VII. Company Commanders will ensure that their Runners are acquainted with the position of Bn. H.Q. & also other Company H.Q.

VIII. Periscopes and Very Pistols, Cups for firing Mill's Grenades will be taken into the line and are not to be handed over as Trench Stores.

IX. S.O.S.Signal must always be in possession of the Company Commander.

X. All Stores such as Officers'Mess Kit and Signalling Equipment for taking into the line, will be stacked at stage on roadway at 7.15 p.m. ready for loading. Transport Officer will arrange to have two limbers for conveyance of this Kit.
Officer's Servants will accompany these Wagons and be responsable for getting the Mess Kit to the Battalion and Company H.Qs.
Signalling Officer will send a N.C.O. to guard Signalling Stores.

XI. Company Commanders will personally warn their men as to place of parade and time and inform them that they are for duty in the Trenches. Certificates that this has been done will be rendered by 4.0 p.m.

XII As soon as Companies have taken over they will report numbers of Picks and Shovels taken over.

Field.   R.B.WEBSTER. Lieut.A/Adjt.
25th July 1918.   26th Bn: Royal Welch Fusiliers.

Secret   OPERATION ORDERS XXXVII
                                    by   Appendix E
                         Lt Colonel H.H.Lee D.S.O.

1. Relief
            The 26th R.W.Fusiliers will be relieved
    in the line by 25th Kings Liverpool Regt on the
    night of the 31st July/1st August 1918.

2. Disposition
            On relief the Battalion will occupy
    the Buckfield System of Trenches M.27.
    The disposition of Companies will be the same
    as that of 25 Kings Liverpool Reg. Viz.
            "A" Coy will occupy Trenches now held
    by the   Q Coy.
            "D"   Coy   "   "   B Coy
            "C"   "   "   "   C Coy
            "B"   "   "   "   D Coy

3. Guides
            One guide per platoon and four
    from Batt. H.Qrs will report at Batt
    H.Qrs at 6 p.m.
            After conducting the 25 Kings
    Liverpool Regt Platoons into the line these
    guides will conduct their own platoons
    to their new positions in Buckfield
    area.

4. Stores
            All maps, Lewis Gun plates,
    defence schemes, trench stores etc will

be handed over on relief and receipts
obtained. These receipts will be forwarded
to Battalion H.Q. by 9.0 a.m. 1st August

5. **Patrols**

The Battalion will furnish all Patrols
for the night 31 July/1st August.

6. **Taking-over**

Major Eyre and one N.C.O. per Coy
and one from H.Qrs will proceed to 7/8th
King's [batt.] H.Qrs at 2:30 p.m. 31st July for
the purpose of taking over.

7. **Relief**

Completion of relief on arriving at
Battalion Area will be reported to Batt
H.Q. the code word for each Coy being
the name of the Coy Commander.

8. **Lewis Guns**

Lewis Guns will be carried up
by hand.

9. **Rations**

Rations will be dumped at S.2.b.9.3.
Companies will send parties to draw their
rations on arrival at their destinations

10. **Kits**

After dumping rations, their
limbers will proceed to dump near
dump ("C" Coys cookhouse) for the purpose
of picking up Officers mess kits &c.

Field
30/7/18

P. M. Clarke
Lt. A/Adjt
Comm' 26th Bn Royal [Fus.]

Army Form C. 2118.

WAR DIARY

INTELLIGENCE SUMMARY.

(Erase heading not required.)

Place	Date	Hour	Summary of Events and Information	Remarks and references to Appendices

ORIGINAL.

Confidential

WAR DIARY

2/Rl. Innis. Nell Fusiliers

From August 1915
To

WAR DIARY
or
INTELLIGENCE SUMMARY

Army Form C. 2118.

Place	Date	Hour	Summary of Events and Information	Remarks and references to Appendices
LINE NEAR MERCATEL	1-8-18	7am	Battalion took over the night support position of the Divisional Sector at 52b (Sheet 51B 2ai). Relief slightly delayed by shelling on some of main communication trenches. Casualties nil during Relief. Weather good.	M.S.
"	2-8-18		Day shelling of position with 5·9s & 4·2s. One Officer and 2 wounded. Weather good. Chérisim near XXXVII	M/A/20 M.S.
"	3-8-18		Again shelling of position and Batt HQ with heavy shell. Weather poor. Trenches wet. At 10pm Battalion was beginning to move over to 11th Regt Scot Fusiliers. Night wet and some shelling on roads and delay entailed. Battalion reported relief complete at 3·30am on 3/8/18 and marched back to BLAIRVILLE QUARRY where arrived by light railway. Casualties = one killed (Shrapnel)	M.S. M.S.
BARLY			One severely wounded (since died) Arrived at siding near BARLY at 9am & marched into billets. Battalion rested and did internal economy.	
"	4-8-18		Battalion carried out Internal Economy. Weather fine.	M.S.
"	5-8-18		Battalion carried out Training for six hours. Weather rain to fair.	
"	6-8-18		Battalion carried out training. Weather variable.	M.S.
"	7-8-18		Battalion inspected by GOC VI Corps Lt General Sir Aylmer Haldane KCB TGO in morning and attended a Trench Bullet demonstration in afternoon. GOC 59th Division listened to officers of evening on Routine War Care of Men in Line. Bgde Order 121 received 6·35pm. Order XXIV at 11pm. Issued Batt Operation	M.S.

2353 Wt. W2544/1454 700,000 5/15 D.D. & L.   A.D.S.S./Forms/C. 2118.

WAR DIARY
or
INTELLIGENCE SUMMARY.
(Erase heading not required.)

Army Form C. 2118.

Place	Date	Hour	Summary of Events and Information	Remarks and references to Appendices
BARLY	8-8-18		Battalion returned during day for line and paraded at 5pm in fighting order. Strength 20 officers 587 OR including rear details. Marched by light Railway following XXX miles BAPAUME—HAPLINCOURT and bivouacked at 6/w9. Left point at 8.30pm. Arrived MARCHEZRAH 9-30 p.m. Battalion bivouacked from 10 till 11 p.m. Somerset Light Infantry Picket by 12-35 AM. 9-6-18 in left sub-sector of 59th Division (Front Northampton) Casualty — one officer rank killed, two wounded.	108
line near MERCATEL	(9-6-18)			
"	9-8-18		Nothing unusual to report on Battalion front. Weather fine. Enemy's artillery active & missing front lines from 4 am to 5 am 10/8/18. Enemy aeroplane close to front lines shot by 9/B.C. and crashed ammunition. Some rifles - pulled one - wounded one.	12 A&C
"	10-8-18		Enemy artillery active at times during above (4—5am). Very normal. Weather fine. Casualty two ranks & H.A. Retaliation carried out.	12A
"	11-8-18		Day normal. Some early morning aeroplane activity. Retaliation carried out from 12 to 1 a.m. Ration Dump shelled at night resulting in wagons being damaged. Casualty - one two ranks wounded. We fire fairly quiet.	12AS
"	12-6-18		Day normal and quiet. Weather fine. Very quiet night with some shelling in early morning 13/8/18 at CATHARMAN-NEWELL precaution on leave. Casualties - Three Other ranks wounded.	12S

Wt W2544/T454 700,000 5/15 D. D. & L. A.D.S.S./(Forms)/C. 2118.

WAR DIARY
or
INTELLIGENCE SUMMARY.
(Erase heading not required.)

Army Form C. 2118.

Place	Date	Hour	Summary of Events and Information	Remarks and references to Appendices
AVRE NEAR MERICOURT	13-8-18		Day normal. Weather fine. Visiting musical torpedo. Wounded = one stretcher. Bgde Order No 122 received extending of battalion by 25' King's Liverpool Regt. Batt. Operation Order No XXI issued	TPWS APPENDIX
	14-8-18		Day normal and enemy very quiet. On superior of Bgdr Gen. Craig 176th Infy Bgde four officers were running patrols left lines at dusk to gain contact with enemy. Result very poor. Enemy found to hold line by strong machine gun posts only. 2/Lt P. BLEASDALE, J.C. TRIGG, ROLAND & Lt T.WOOD TESSONNA did good work. Relieved by 25' King's Liverpool by 12-35 am 15/8/18.	TPWS
BRETENCOURT	15-8-18	5-15am	Last platoon of battalion arrived in billets. Batt. HD in CHATEAU. Capt R.J.BUNTING 2/6 Sherwood Foresters reported for duty. Lieut (A/Capt) R.B.WEBSTER relinquished appointment of adjutant. Capt R.J. BUNTING appointed adjutant 15/8/18. Battalion ordered cleaners and one hour's drill. Weather fine. Casualties = nil.	TPWS
"	16-8-18		Battalion trained over six hours. Weather fine. Casualties = nil	TPWS
	17-8-18		Battalion carried out alarm assembly at 5-30 pm & marched in full kit to billets. Returned to billets 11-45 pm. Training carried out for six hours during day. Weather fine. Cloudy at night. Casualties = nil.	TPWS

Army Form C. 2118.

WAR DIARY
or
INTELLIGENCE SUMMARY.
(Erase heading not required.)

Instructions regarding War Diaries and Intelligence Summaries are contained in F. S. Regs., Part II. and the Staff Manual respectively. Title pages will be prepared in manuscript.

Place	Date	Hour	Summary of Events and Information	Remarks and references to Appendices
BRETENCOURT	18-8-18		Battalion rested. Weather fine. Casualties = Nil.	Appx 5.
"	19-8-18		Battalion carried out Training. Weather fine. Bgde. Order No 123 received. Casualties = Nil.	Appx 5.
"	20-8-18		Battalion Issued Operation Order No. 2. Proceeded at 8 p.m. and marched to CHAT MAIGRE & took over left support line. Weather fine. Casualties = Nil.	Appx F.
CHAT MAIGRE SUPPORT NEAR MERCATEL	21-8-18		Day quiet. Weather fine. Casualties = O.R. Davies wounded. one.	Appx G.
	22-8-18		Day quiet. B.B. preparations for attack. No enemy in Aveluy. pHing 5-6 p.m. Weather very fine. Casualties = nil.	Appx 5.
	23-8-18		Heavy bombardment of enemy lines at 3.15 a.m. increasing to drum fire which lifted at 7 a.m. opposite MERCATEL sector when 52nd DIV. went over the top. Working party of 40.O.R. ½ 2nd Lieut. P. Bleasdale joined while working in communication French. Weather fine but became overcast as the day wore on. Battalion withdrawn from CHAT MAIGRE at 10.30 p.m. Rendezvous at Mill BRETENCOURT. No casualties during withdrawal.	Appx H.

2353 Wt. W2544/1454 700,000 5/15 D. D. & L.   A.D.S.S./Forms/C. 2118.

Army Form C. 2118.

WAR DIARY
or
INTELLIGENCE SUMMARY.
(Erase heading not required.)

Instructions regarding War Diaries and Intelligence Summaries are contained in F. S. Regs., Part II. and the Staff Manual respectively. Title pages will be prepared in manuscript.

Place	Date	Hour	Summary of Events and Information	Remarks and references to Appendices
SAULTY	24-8-18		Marched to SAULTY 12.20 a.m. Bivouaced in field 4 a.m. (about 1500 yds from Railway Station) Entrained 5 p.m. Weather overcast.	Appx.
St HILAIRE - COTTES	25-8-18		Arrived LILLERS 5 a.m. Detrained and marched to St HILAIRE - COTTES, arriving 7 a.m. Battalion rested. Weather variable.	Appx B.
LA PIERRIERE	26-8-18		Battalion carried out Internal Economy and one hours drill during the forenoon. Moved to LA PIERRIERE at 2.50 p.m. and relieved 10th Buffs in reserve. Arrival 7 p.m. Weather variable.	Appx B
	27-8-18		Battalion carried out training. Weather fine.	Appx
	28-8-18		Battalion carried out training. Weather fine.	Appx
	29-8-18		Battalion carried out training. Weather fine.	Appx

2353 Wt. W2544/1454 700,000 5/15 D. D. & L. A.D.S.S./Forms/C. 2118.

Army Form C. 2118.

WAR DIARY
or
INTELLIGENCE SUMMARY.
(Erase heading not required.)

Place	Date	Hour	Summary of Events and Information	Remarks and references to Appendices
LA PERRIERE	30-8-18		Battalion carried out training. Weather variable.	
	31-8-18		Battalion carried out training. Moved to Asylum St VENANT at 5.20 p.m. taking over from 11th ROYAL SCOTS 7th 5/15 E.P.S. Weather fine.	

SECRET.

OPERATION ORDER NO. XXXIX.
by
Lieut-Colonel H.H.Lee D.S.O.
Commanding 26th Royal Welch Fusiliers.

No......

Map Ref.
Sheet 51c
51b

7th August 1918.

I. RELIEF.
The 26th Royal Welch Fusiliers will relieve the 11th Bn. Somerset Light Infantry in the front line system of the left Divisional Subsector on the night of 8/9th August, 1918.

II. ADVANCE PARTIES.
1 Officer (who must have had previous experience in line) and 1 N.C.O. per Company, and 2/lieut. H.A.WARDIE with 1 N.C.O. from Bn. H.Q., will parade at Brigade H.Q. at 8.45 a.m. and will be conveyed by motor lorry to the line and will take over from corresponding Companies of Somerset Light Infantry.

III. DISPOSITION IN LINE.
"A" Company will occupy the right sector of front line with 2 platoons, with one platoon in Wren Support and 1 platoon in Stable Picquet.
"B" Company will occupy the left sector of front line with 2 platoons, with 1 platoon in Sunken Road near Aid Post and 1 platoon in post near Crucifix.
"C" Company will occupy right sector of reserve line with 1 platoon in Teak Trench.
"D" Company will occupy left sector of reserve line.

IV. PARADE.
The Battalion will parade on the road outside billets in fighting order, with greatcoats rolled over haversacks, and water bottles filled at 6.0 p.m. and march to B.C. 100P (P23.d.82) where they will entrain.
Order of March :-
Battalion H.Q.
"A" Company.
"B"   "
"C"   "
"D" Company.
The Lewis guns will be conveyed to B.C.100P in limbered wagons. In detraining they will be carried by hand into the line. Each Coy. will take its full complement of Lewis guns.

V. GUIDES.
Guides from 11th S.L.I. will meet the Battalion at MARBLE ARCH and conduct platoons into the line.

VI.
2/lieut. W.KEITH will report to Staff Captain at B.C. 100P at 11.30 a.m., 8th August.

VII. RATIONS.
Rations for the 9th instant will be cooked on 8th and carried by men into the line.

VIII.
Tommy Cookers will be issued to "A" and "B" Companies to enable them to heat their rations. They will be packed in the Company Dixies.

IX.
Officers' Mess Kit and cooking utensils, and filled petrol tins will be conveyed to Battn. Dump near Aid Post by transport.
Mess kit and cooking utensils will be stacked ready for loading at Q.M.Stores by 2.45 p.m. On arrival Companies will detail parties to proceed immediately to the Battn.Dump for the purpose of drawing there mess kit, cooking utensils and water.

X.
Defence Schemes, programmes of work, maps, aeroplane photos, trench stores, reserve ammunition and bombs etc., will be taken over, receipts given and lists forwarded to Bn. H.Q. by 9.0 a.m. 9th August.

XI.
Each water cart will be brought up filled on alternate nights and remain near Aid Post for 24 hours.
O.C. Platoons in the Sunken Road, will be responsible that it is properly camouflaged.

P.T.O.

- 2 -

XII   Officers' valises, men's packs and such surplus kit as may not be required in the line will be stacked at Q.M.Stores at 4.0 p.m.

XIII   The Quartermasters' Stores and Transport lines will not move. Advance Transport, detail of which will be issued later, will proceed to BESTENCOURT.

XIV   Companies will report completion of relief to Battalion H.Q. Code word - "NIL RETURN".

                                       R.S.WEBSTER. Captain & Adjutant.
                                       26th Royal Welch Fusiliers.

Operation Order XL
by
Lieut-Colonel H H Lee D.S.O.
Commanding 26th Royal Welch Fusrs.

11th August 1918.

RELIEF

"A" and "B" Companies will relieve their Front Line Platoons by those in Support, tonight, under Company arrangements.

Completion of relief to be signalled to Bn. H.Q. Code-word "RAT."

Patrol tonight will be found by reserve Companies.

Men of "C" Company attached to "B" Company will remain in the Front Line tonight and be relieved tomorrow.

Field
11·8·1918

Capt. & Adjt.
26th Royal Welch Fusiliers

OPERATION ORDERS XLII
by
Lieut-Colonel H.H.Lee D.S.O.
Cmg. 26th Battalion Royal Welch Fusiliers.

I. The 26th Bn. Royal Welch Fusiliers will relieve the 17th Royal Sussex Regt. in CHAT HAIGH area tonight.

II. One officer per company and one from H.Q. will reconnoitre the position this afternoon. Companies will occupy the corresponding posts of the company of the same letter in the 17th Royal Sussex Regt. and platoons will occupy positions held by corresponding platoons.

III. Battalion will parade at 8 p.m. and proceed by companies to R.29.d.0.8 200 yards distance between companies. There companies will break up into platoons at 100 yards distance.
Lewis Gun Limbers will accompany companies to where Lewis Guns will be unloaded.

IV. Officers Mess Kit, Signalling Stores, Cooking Pots etc. will be stacked outside Q.M. Stores at 7 p.m. ready for loading.

V. Officers Valises will be stacked at Q.M. Stores at 5 p.m. for removal to RAPLY.

VI. Rations for the 21st will be carried cooked by the men.
Water Bottles will be filled.
The Limbers containing petrol tins filled, Officers Mess Kit and Company Dixies will accompany companies.

VII. All defence schemes, aeroplane photographs, programmes of work in progress, secret maps, stores, reserve ammunition, bombs etc. will be taken over and receipts given. Copies of these receipts are to be handed in Orderly Room at 10 a.m. the 21st inst.

VIII. Completion of relief will be notified to Batt. H.Q. by message "Nil Return".

IX. At night equipment must be worn by all ranks in CHAT HAIGH area.

X. Blankets and packs will be stacked at Q.M. Stores at 4 p.m. by companies.

XI. Companies will vacate their huts at 5 p.m.

H.J.Bunting.
Capt. & Adjutant.
26th Bn. Royal Welch Fusiliers.

20-6-18.

Operation Order XLIII
by
Lieut-Colonel H.H. LEE D.S.O.
Commanding 26th Bn. ROYAL WELCH FUSILIERS.
===

(I). The 26th Bn. Royal Welch Fusiliers will relieve the 10th Buffs in reserve at LA PERRIERE today

(II) Route:- BOURECQ - LILLERS - BUSNES.

(III) The Battalion will form up ready to march off at 2.50 p.m. in following order:-

Headquarters
"A" Company
"B"   "
"C"   "
"D"   "

Head of Headquarters to be at road junction T.6.c.1.1.

(IV). Transport will accompany battalion. The Company transport following each Company. The remainder in rear of Battalion.

(V). Dress:- Marching order with packs. Orders re Blankets will be issued later.

(VI) Billetting party consisting of Lt. Wardle with 1 N.C.O. per Company will report to O.C. 10th Buffs by 11.45 a.m. They will proceed on bicycles.

(VII) All kits and stores ready for loading will be stacked outside billets by 12.30 p.m. The Transport officer will arrange to collect them.

(VIII) Only authorized kits will be carried on the Transport. All surplus Officers' kit, stores, etc., will be dumped at under a guard of 1 N.C.O. and 5 men

Field   K.J. BUNTING.   Capt. & Adjutant.

26.8.18   26th ROYAL WELCH FUSILIERS

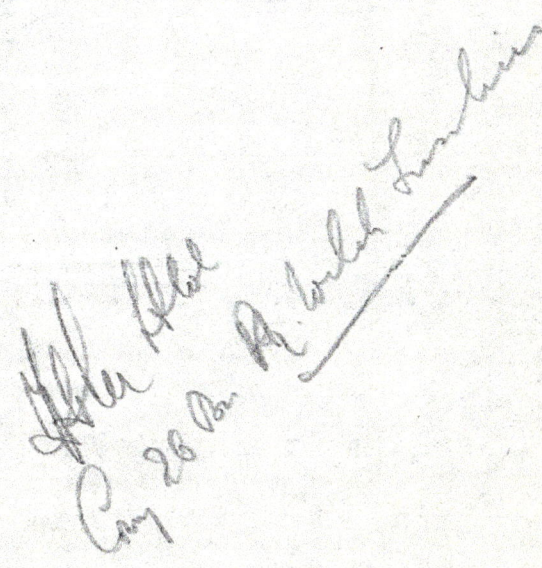

Army Form C. 2118.

WAR DIARY
or
INTELLIGENCE SUMMARY.

(Erase heading not required.)

CONFIDENTIAL

WAR DIARY
26th Rgt. Welch Fus.
September — 1918.
VOL. XXVII

WAR DIARY or INTELLIGENCE SUMMARY

Army Form C. 2118.

Place	Date	Hour	Summary of Events and Information	Remarks and references to Appendices
ASYLUM St VENANT	1-9-18		Battalion rested. Weather fine.	App.B
	2-9-18		Battalion inspected by General Birdwood. Training carried out during afternoon. Weather variable	App.B
Q6c.32.96 Sheet 36A	3-9-18		Battalion relieved 11th Bn Somerset Light Infantry. No casualties. Battalion in support. Weather fine. Operation Order XLIV issued	App.B Appendix "A"
	4-9-18		Battalion moved up to P.14.a.5.9. Sheet 36A at dawn. Moved up to LESTREM at 3pm. Weather from cloudy & dull. No casualties	App.B
LESTREM	5-9-18		Battalion still at LESTREM in support. No casualties. Weather variable and stormy. Nothing special to report	App.B
	6-9-18			App.B
	7-9-18	2.30pm	Battalion still in support but moved up to neighbourhood of RIEZ-BAILLEUL. B.H.Q. at Weather stormy. No casualties. Nothing special to report.	App.B
	8-9-18		No change	App.B
	9-9-18		Battalion relieved Northumberland Fusiliers in front line. No casualties during day. Weather very stormy. (Operation Order XLV issued)	App.B Appendix A
	10-9-18 11-9-18 12-9-18		Day quiet on front. Nothing unusual occurrence. Operation Order XLVI issued. Day quiet. Nothing unusual to report. Enemy raided post No "B" Coy near PICANTIN. Raid was driven off by five 5 followed u/s. Two wounded prisoners taken. Vt.W.z341/1451 a Aug.18 700,000 5/15 D.D. & L. A.D.S.S./Forms/C.2148. One subsequently reported killed but the other behaved well.	App.B Appendix "B" App.B

Army Form C. 2118.

WAR DIARY
or
INTELLIGENCE SUMMARY.
(Erase heading not required.)

Instructions regarding War Diaries and Intelligence Summaries are contained in F.S. Regs., Part II. and the Staff Manual respectively. Title pages will be prepared in manuscript.

Place	Date	Hour	Summary of Events and Information	Remarks and references to Appendices
PICANTIN	13-9-18	8.15 pm	Relief by 11th Somerset Light Infantry commenced. Relief complete by 2 am 14-9-18. Weather variable but fair. Lieut R.B.WEBSTER rejoined from leave.	PGS.
PONT RIQUEUL	14-9-18	2 am	Battalion took over rest billets in village ruins and neighbourhood. Weather fair. Slight harassing from hostile H.P. for night	PGS.
"	15-9-18		Battalion bathed at Corps baths near AIRE & carried out internal economy. Weather fine.	PGS.
"	16-9-18		Battalion employed on road clearing and little repair. Some training carried out. Weather fine.	PGS.
"	17-9-18		Battalion engaged on road repair. Some training carried out. Weather fine.	PGS.
"	18-9-18		Battalion engaged on road repair. Some training carried out. Weather fine.	PGS.
"	19-9-18		Battalion engaged on road repair. Some training. Weather fine.	PGS.
"	20-9-18		Battalion engaged on road repair. Some training. Weather fine.	PGS.
"	21-9-18		Battalion engaged on road repair. Camp visually shelled during afternoon, evening and night by H.V. Gun. and A.23. Billets vacated as precautionary measure. Weather wet in forenoon, improving to fine.	PGS.

Army Form C. 2118.

WAR DIARY
or
INTELLIGENCE SUMMARY.
(Erase heading not required.)

Instructions regarding War Diaries and Intelligence Summaries are contained in F. S. Regs., Part II. and the Staff Manual respectively. Title pages will be prepared in manuscript.

Place	Date	Hour	Summary of Events and Information	Remarks and references to Appendices
PONT RIQUEUL	22-9-18	2.30pm	Batt. HQ. moved to new location in PONT RIQUEUL. Weather fine. — storm rain in morning. Lieut. H.W. TREGURNA rejoined from leave. 2nd Lieut. G.S. BECK (granted 14 days Special Leave) proceeded.	R&S
"	23-9-18		Battalion carried out road repair and billet improvement. Weather fine.	R&S
"	24-9-18		Battalion carried out billet improvement and some training. Weather fine	R&S
"	25-9-18		The following reported for duty 2/Lt- H.L. ELLIS, A.E. COLLINS, H.E. WILLIAMS, T.E. WHITELEG, R.G. THOMAS, all Royal Welch Fusiliers. Battalion on bathing and billet improvement. Weather fine.	R&S
"	26-9-18		Battalion carried out training. Weather fine.	R&S
"	27-9-18		Battalion carried out training. Weather fine. 2/Lieut. M.V. COLLINS (R.W.F.) reported for duty.	R&S
"	28-9-18	6.15pm	Battalion marched out of billets to take over left Subsector of Illuvisual Front in relief of 35th Northumberland Fusiliers. Operation Order No. XLIX. Relief complete 1.am 28/29th Sept.	R&S Appendix "C"
"	29-9-18		Day normal. Heavy shelling along front at times. Battalion relieved from front line by 2.5th Kings Liverpool Regt. and 17th Royal Sussex Regt. Casualties - Other Ranks died of wounds - one; wounded - four. Weather - variable very wet at night. Operation Order No. L issued.	R&S Appendix "D"

Army Form C. 2118.

WAR DIARY
or
INTELLIGENCE SUMMARY.
(Erase heading not required.)

Instructions regarding War Diaries and Intelligence Summaries are contained in F. S. Regs., Part II. and the Staff Manual respectively. Title pages will be prepared in manuscript.

Place	Date	Hour	Summary of Events and Information	Remarks and references to Appendices
R.5 (Sheet 36A)	30-9-18	2am	Battalion occupied billets in neighbourhood — with two Companies forward — one in CARTER'S POST and one in MUDDY LANE POST. Battalion bathed at RIEZ BAILLEUL. Weather fine.	TROOPS

W/ for B. W. Kilorel
Cmdg. 26th R.4.5F.

Operation Order No. XLIV.
by
Lieut-Colonel H.H. LEE, D.S.O.,
Commanding 26th Bn. ROYAL WELCH FUSILIERS.
===

Appendix A*

The Battn. will relieve 11th Bn. Somerset Light Infantry in support today.

Coys. will parade ready to march off at 11.45 a.m., dress fighting kit with greatcoats, waterbottles filled.

Coys. will relieve corresponding Coys. of Somerset Light Infantry.

Cookers will be taken into the line.

Officers' Valises will not be taken.

Officers' Mess kit and Lewis Guns will be loaded by 11.30 a.m.

Coy. Transport will accompany Companies.

Coys. will march as follows:-
    200 yards between Coys.
    100 yards between platoons

Water carts filled will accompany Battalion.

All Officers' Valises, men's packs, and blankets will be stored in Q.M. Stores by 11 a.m.

Pack Mules will accompany Battn.

Field
3.9.18.

K.J. BUNTING, Capt. & Adjutant.
26th Bn. ROYAL WELCH FUSILIERS.

To Recipients of
    Tonight's Orders.

            Para 5. 1st line.   Amend to read, "The
present billets of "D" Company"

            Para 7. 4th line.   Amend to read, "Advance
parties and 1 guide per Company.

                                K.J.BUNTING, Capt. & Adjt.
    2.9.18   26th ROYAL WELCH FUSILIERS

Operation Order XLIX.
by
Lieut-Colonel H.H.LEE, D.S.O.,
Commanding 26th Bn. ROYAL WELCH FUSILIERS.

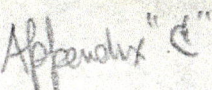 Appendix "C"

The Battalion will relieve the 36th Bn. Northumberland Fusiliers in the Line tonight, in the left front sub-sector.

"A" Coy. will be right front Company.
"B" Coy. will be left front Company.
"C" Coy. will be right support Company
"D" Coy. will be left Support Company

Parties will proceed to reconnoitre the line at once.

Companies will move as follows:-

Battn. H.Q. at 6.15 p.m.   )   PONT RICQUEL-L.36.a.82
"A" Company follows Bn. H.Q.)   -G.31.b.70- MUDDY LANE-
"B"   "   follows "A" Coy.) route.   No. 1 Road.
"C"   "   follows "B" Coy.)   Guides meet platoons
"D"   "   follows "C" Coy.)   M.5.a.41

Mens packs and blankets and Officers' Kits will be ready stacked at Billets by 5 p.m.
Transport Officer will arrange to convey them to the Brigade Dump.

Rations for tomorrow to be cooked at once and carried on the man.
Tommy Cookers will be issued to Companies as follows :-

"A" Company)
"B"   "   )
"C"   "   ) 50 per Company.
"D"   "   )

Lewis Gun Limbers will accompany Companies following in rear of the leading platoon.

One hundred yards will be maintained between platoons.

All Aeroplane photos, Defence Schemes, and Trench Stores will be taken over and receipts given.

Officers Mess Kit will be ready for loading outside Billets at 5 P.m. Officers Mess Kit must be reduced to a minimum.

Battn. H.Q. HARLECH CASTLE.

R. Gleinden
Capt A/Adjt.
26th Bn. ROYAL WELCH FUSILIERS.

28.9.18

Army Form C. 2118.

WAR DIARY
or
INTELLIGENCE SUMMARY.

(Erase heading not required.)

Instructions regarding War Diaries and Intelligence Summaries are contained in F. S. Regs., Part II. and the Staff Manual respectively. Title pages will be prepared in manuscript.

Place	Date	Hour	Summary of Events and Information	Remarks and references to Appendices

Confidential

WAR DIARY
26th R.W.F.
October 1st – 31st 1918
Volume XXVIII

Original

Army Form C. 2118.

No. 76/59

Vol 4

WAR DIARY
or
INTELLIGENCE SUMMARY.
(Erase heading not required.)

Army Form C. 2118.

Place	Date	Hour	Summary of Events and Information	Remarks and references to Appendices
R5 (Sheet 36A)	1.10.18		Battalion carried out training. Weather fine	BAJ.
	2.10.18	8 AM	Battalion passed under orders of 178th Infy Bgde. Ordered into line to take over left sector of 61st Divisional Front from at MOEUVRES. Battalion embussed at buses at 7 p.m. & proceeded in relief of Premier Regt. Casualties Other Ranks - two killed - three NYD	RSM
BAC ST MAUR	3.10.18		Battalion commenced pursuit of enemy who are falling back towards LILLE. First objective reached and Second objective PEAR TREE FARM nearly attained but being held back in aft by M.G. fire cops retired to first objective for night and dug only a screen near second objective. Casualties - Other ranks wounded - one.	RMJ
LAVESSEE POST	4.10.18		Pursuit of the enemy continued at 5.0 am the second objective being from PEAR TREE FARM to S.W. of the village of WEZ MACQUART. Two objectives were reached about 3.0 p.m. after being held up on the left flank by M.G. fire. The battalion then moved into the old trench from two records for the night play, who were the centre company were ordered to push forward and establish a line on the German old front line (WIDENT TRENCH) so as to form a complete defensive line from PEAR TREE FARM to REZUMS	B.
"	5.10.18			

Army Form C. 2118.

WAR DIARY
or
INTELLIGENCE SUMMARY.
(Erase heading not required.)

Instructions regarding War Diaries and Intelligence Summaries are contained in F.S. Regs., Part II. and the Staff Manual respectively. Title pages will be prepared in manuscript.

Place	Date	Hour	Summary of Events and Information	Remarks and references to Appendices
Ration (?)				
PEAR TREE FARM	5.10.16		Casualties 2 O.R. killed 3 wounded. Fine day.	CO
"	6.10.16		Battalion relieved by 14th Batt. Royal Sussex Regiment. Relief complete 3.0 am. Battalion returned to billets in Pereuse Boston along FLEURBAIX	CO
			PORMENTIERS ROAD	
L'ARMÉE POST	7.10.16		Battalion resting. Lt. Col. N.W. GARDNER took over command from Major	CO
			F. FYFE	
do	8.10.16		Inspection of A and B Coys by Lt. Col. N.W. GARDNER	CO
do	9.10.16		Training carried out.	CO
do	10.10.16		Training carried out.	CO
FERME DE BUZ	11.10.16		Battalion relieved 14th Bn. Royal Sussex Regt. in front line. "B" & "C" Coys	CO
			in firing line, "D" Coy support & "A" Coy reserve	
do	12.10.16		Line of observation re-adjusted by Commanding Officer. Posts put in to a total of 9	(2nd)
			defence	(3rd)
do	13.10.16		Enemy very alert. Patrols report the front (R.21) heavily held by enemy m.g.	(3rd)
do	14.10.16		Having orders to proceed forward relieved "A" & "D" Coys relieved "B" & "C" Coys in firing	Appendix A
			line. Batt. Operation Order No. 53 issued	(3rd)

Army Form C. 2118.

WAR DIARY
or
INTELLIGENCE SUMMARY.

(Erase heading not required.)

Instructions regarding War Diaries and Intelligence Summaries are contained in F. S. Regs., Part II. and the Staff Manual respectively. Title pages will be prepared in manuscript.

Place	Date	Hour	Summary of Events and Information	Remarks and references to Appendices
do	15/10/18		Patrols report enemy withdrawal. Batt pushed forward at 17.30 hrs & gained 1st objective. 3 O.Rs in same for the night. 2/Lt Simpson wounded.	(1)
do	16/10/18		Move forward again at 05.30 hrs and gained 2nd objective INADEQUATE TRENCH at 11 hrs. Gained INADEQUATE TRENCH for the night. Spent very quiet. Enemy appears to have gone back a considerable distance.	(2)
MARQUETTE	17/10/18		Battalion again moved at 07.30 hrs. The third objective MARQUETTE gained without opposition. The inhabitants gave the troops an enthusiastic reception.	(3)
RECUIL	19/10/18		Battalion advanced crossing LILLE canal by R.E. Footbridge near MARQUETTE and proceeded east. Near LES LAURIERS (Q.29 (TOUSSAINT) contact gained with enemy troops. Patrols pressed forward through RECUIL to HEMPENPONT. "B" Coy entered at 1700 hrs but was withdrawn at dusk. Heavy enemy shelling at HEM CHURCH and W. END of HEMPENPONT. Gas shells Between RECUIL and HEMPENPONT at 1730 hrs. Battalion formed outposts on south side of MARCQ river & was in touch with flank units. B.M 349 (Byde Order) received	F.S.W.
SAILLY-LEZ-LANNOY	19/10/18		Advance resumed. MARCQ crossed east and west of HEMPENPONT. Moved through HEM to line of LANNOY - FOREST HILLE Railway. 25th Kings (Liverpool) Regt coming up relieved and passed through eastward. Batt marched into SAILLY-LEZ-LANNOY & billetted. Batt was in Byde Reserve after 12.00 hrs. Byde Order B.M. 363 received	P.S.W.
	20/10/18		Battalion marched to HOLAIN's & billeted.	F8303

Army Form C. 2118.

WAR DIARY
or
INTELLIGENCE SUMMARY.
(Erase heading not required.)

Instructions regarding War Diaries and Intelligence Summaries are contained in F. S. Regs., Part II. and the Staff Manual respectively. Title pages will be prepared in manuscript.

Place	Date	Hour	Summary of Events and Information	Remarks and references to Appendices
HOLANS	21-10-18		Remained in billets.	Plans
"	22-10-18		196th Infty Bgde relieved by 177th Infty Bgde. Battalion relieved by 15th Essex Regt. at 14.00 hrs & marched back and billeted in TOUFFLERS. Bgde Order No 138 received.	Plans
TOUFFLERS	23-10-18		Baths and cleaning under Coy- arrangements	Plans
"	24-10-18		Baths and cleaning.	Plans
"	25-10-18		Training and cleaning.	Plans
"	26-10-18		Training.	Plans
"	27-10-18		Divine Service.	Plans
"	28-10-18		Training.	Plans
"	29-10-18		Training.	Plans
"	30-10-18		Training.	Plans
"	31-10-18	0900	176th Infty Bgde inspected by G.O.C. 59th Division. Military Medals presented to :- Sgt (47250) DELANEY, 57506 Sgt. CORDEN A, 27552 Pte McCOWAN, 26680 4/Cpl ROBERTS, 82315 Sgt Major PORTER, 71964 Pte WILLIAMSON, 82151 4/Cpl KING, 57521 Pte GLOVER. BAR TO MILITARY MEDAL to :- 82215 Pte LARGE. The following have been awarded MILITARY MEDAL but have not/received. 42527 Pte T. GORE, 46940 T. WEBSTER 37791 Sgt. GRINDLEY.	Plans

N Gardner Lt
Col. 26th R.S.F. 2/XI/1918

Army Form C. 2118.

WAR DIARY
or
INTELLIGENCE SUMMARY.
(Erase heading not required.)

N.b. Gentot H.S.T. 2/11/1918
Coly 26' R.A.F.

WAR DIARY

26TH Battalion

Royal Welch Fus.

Volume XXX

November 1918.

CONFIDENTIAL

WAR DIARY
or
INTELLIGENCE SUMMARY.

(Erase heading not required.)

Army Form C. 2118.

Place	Date	Hour	Summary of Events and Information	Remarks and references to Appendices
TOUFFLERS	1-11-18		Training	P35
"	2-11-18		Heavy drum fire at dawn to N.E.	P45
"	3-11-18		Divine Service Parades	P45
"	4-11-18		Training	P45
"	5-11-18		Training	P45
"	6-11-18		Training	P&S
"	7-11-18		Training	P45
"	8-11-18	1530	Word recd billeted in environs of CHASS east of TOUFFLERS. 176R Inf Bgde becomes Back up Sft-foot	P45
CHASS	9-11-18	1015	Battalion moved forward as the enemy has evacuated right bank of SCHELDT. "Battalion crossed" near PERD by Pontondge and advanced in support of 178R Infy Bgde. Billeted in GRAND REST	Rgbt
GRAND REST	10-11-18	8/00	Moved from GRAND REST and ultimately billeted in DELPRE NW of VELAINES by dusk	Rg.N
DELPRE	11-11-18	1200	Armistice announced. Battalion remained in billets.	Rg.S
"	12-11-18	0900	Battalion marched out and billeted at GRAND REST	P45
GRAND REST	13-11-18		Some training & sports	Rgw
"	14-11-18	1050	Marched out and billeted in MOURCOURT	P45

WAR DIARY
or
INTELLIGENCE SUMMARY.
(Erase heading not required.)

Army Form C. 2118.

Instructions regarding War Diaries and Intelligence Summaries are contained in F. S. Regs., Part II. and the Staff Manual respectively. Title pages will be prepared in manuscript.

Place	Date	Hour	Summary of Events and Information	Remarks and references to Appendices
MOORCOURT	15-11-18	20/50	Battalion moved west - crossed SCHELDT - & billeted in TEMPLEUVE	Pgs5
TEMPLEUVE	16-11-18	10.15	Battalion moved and billeted in FACHES - THUMESNIL - near LILLE	S+P
THUMESNIL	17-11-18		Scheme training	P3+S
"	18-11-18		Army Education Scheme & Training	P+S
"	19-11-18		Army Education Scheme & Training	P+S
"	20-11-18		Army Education Scheme & Training	P+S
"	21-11-18		Army Education Scheme & Training	P+S
"	22-11-18		Army Education Scheme & Training	P+S
"	23-11-18		176th Infty Bgde Sports.	P+S
"	24-11-18		G.O.C. 59th Division presented ribands Military Cross to 2/Lieut. C.F.TUFFY, 2/Lt. F.W.SIMPSON, Lieut.(A/Capt.)H.W.TREGONNA, and Military Medal to No. 47323 Cpl. G.E.LEWIS, 52169 Pte. W. NASH, 323.25 Pte. E. AYLIFFE, 40340 Pte. J. WEBSTER, 42527 Pte. J. GORE	P+S
"	25-11-18		Army Education Scheme & Training	P+S
"	26-11-18		Army Education Scheme & Training	P+S
"	27-11-18		Army Education Scheme & Training	P+S
"	28-11-18		Army Education Scheme - Holiday	P+S

WAR DIARY
or
INTELLIGENCE SUMMARY.

(Erase heading not required.)

Army Form C. 2118.

Place	Date	Hour	Summary of Events and Information	Remarks and references to Appendices
THUMESNIL	29-1-19		Army Education Scheme of Training	[A]
"	30-1-19		Army Education Scheme of Training	[B]
			N L Gardner Lt. Col.	
			Cdg. 26th Bn Royal Welch Fusiliers	

Army Form C. 2118.

WAR DIARY
or
INTELLIGENCE SUMMARY.
(Erase heading not-required.)

Instructions regarding War Diaries and Intelligence Summaries are contained in F. S. Regs., Part II. and the Staff Manual respectively. Title pages will be prepared in manuscript.

Place	Date	Hour	Summary of Events and Information	Remarks and references to Appendices

A6945 Wt. W14422/M1160 359000 12/16 D. D. & L. Forms/C./2118/14.

Army Form C. 2118.

WAR DIARY
or
INTELLIGENCE SUMMARY.
(Erase heading not required.)

Confidential

War Diary
December 1918
Volume XXXI
26th Batt. Royal Welch Fus.

WAR DIARY
or
INTELLIGENCE SUMMARY.
(*Erase heading not required.*)

Army Form C. 2118.

Instructions regarding War Diaries and Intelligence Summaries are contained in F. S. Regs., Part II. and the Staff Manual respectively. Title pages will be prepared in manuscript.

Place	Date	Hour	Summary of Events and Information	Remarks and references to Appendices
THIMESNIL	1-12-18		Divine Service	
"	2-12-18		Training & Education	
"	3-12-18		Bathing & Education	
"	4-12-18		Route March & Education	
"	5-12-18		Holiday. Transport marched out 0900 en route BARLIN	
"	6-12-18	0930	Battalion entrained for BARLIN. Arrived BARLIN 1500 & billeted in hutment camp	
BARLIN	7-12-18		Camp Improvement	
"	8-12-18		Divine Service	
"	9-12-18		Camp Improvement - some training	
"	10-12-18		Education	
"	11-12-18		Education, Recreational & Military Training	
"	12-12-18		Holiday	
"	13-12-18		Education & Training	
"	14-12-18		Education & Training	
"	15-12-18		Divine Service	
"	16-12-18		Education & Industries	

Army Form C. 2118.

WAR DIARY
or
INTELLIGENCE SUMMARY.
(Erase heading not required.)

Instructions regarding War Diaries and Intelligence Summaries are contained in F. S. Regs., Part II. and the Staff Manual respectively. Title pages will be prepared in manuscript.

Place	Date	Hour	Summary of Events and Information	Remarks and references to Appendices
BAPAUME	17-12-18		Education	BJ
"	18-12-18		Education	BJ
"	19-12-18		Holiday & Salvage	BJ
"	20-12-18		Education & Recreational Training - Salvage	BJ
"	21-12-18		Education - Recreation - Salvage	BJ
"	22-12-18		Divine Service	BJ
"	23-12-18		Education - Recreation - Salvage	BJ
"	24-12-18		Education - Recreation - Salvage	BJ
"	25-12-18		Christmas Day	BJ
"	26-12-18		Recreation - Holiday	BJ
"	27-12-18		Education	BJ
"	28-12-18		Bathing	BJ
"	29-12-18		Divine Service	BJ
"	30-12-18		Education - Recreation oxo Battalion marched out of BAPAUME en route for STYEYCHYT detraining 15:30pm	BJ
"	31-12-18		Education - Recreation 9:00 am Battalion co-rested at YSENT en route for HERSEGHEM detraining 14:00 pm	BJ

McGarthuir Lt-Col
1/1/1919 = 26 O.R. =

A6945 Wt. W1422/M1160 350,000 12/16 D. D. & L. Forms/C./2118/14

Army Form C. 2118.

WAR DIARY
or
INTELLIGENCE SUMMARY.
(Erase heading not required.)

Instructions regarding War Diaries and Intelligence Summaries are contained in F. S. Regs., Part II. and the Staff Manual respectively. Title pages will be prepared in manuscript.

Place	Date	Hour	Summary of Events and Information	Remarks and references to Appendices

A6945 Wt. W14412/M1160 350,000 12/16 D. D. & L. Forms/C/2118/14.

Army Form C. 2118.

WAR DIARY
or
INTELLIGENCE SUMMARY.

(Erase heading not required.)

Instructions regarding War Diaries and Intelligence Summaries are contained in F. S. Regs., Part II. and the Staff Manual respectively. Title pages will be prepared in manuscript.

Place	Date	Hour	Summary of Events and Information	Remarks and references to Appendices

Confidential

War Diary
January 1919
Volume XXXII
26th Batt. Royal Welch Fus.

WAR DIARY
or
INTELLIGENCE SUMMARY.
(Erase heading not required.)

Army Form C. 2118.

Place	Date	Hour	Summary of Events and Information	Remarks and references to Appendices
HONDEGHEM	1-1-19		Battalion in camp at BORRE BECQUE - 2 miles from HONDEGHEM - Preliminary taking over of HONDEGHEM "Demobilisation Staging Camp"	249
"	2-1-19		Improvement of Hutments - Battalion takeover from staff of "Staging Camp"	249
"	3-1-19		Work connected with Staging Camp being carried on	249
"	4-1-19		Work connected with Staging Camp being carried on	249
"	5-1-19		Battalion mostly at work on permanent fatigues in and beyond connected with the "Staging Camp", new being run by Battalion staff entirely	249
"	6-1-19		Work in Staging Camp - general improvement of Hutments	249
"	7-1-19		Work chiefly in Staging Camp being carried on	249
"	8-1-19		Work chiefly in Staging Camp being carried on	249
"	9-1-19		Improvement of Hutments + general work of Staging Camp carried on	249
"	10-1-19		Routine of Staging Camp being carried on - Hours improvement of Hutments	249
"	11-1-19		Routine of Staging Camp carried on. Bathing during day	249
"	12-1-19		Hutments improved & general fatigues done	249
"	13-1-19		Routine of camp performed	249
"	14-1-19		Whole of Battalion on fatigue	249

Army Form C. 2118.

WAR DIARY
or
INTELLIGENCE SUMMARY.
(Erase heading not required.)

Instructions regarding War Diaries and Intelligence Summaries are contained in F. S. Regs., Part II. and the Staff Manual respectively. Title pages will be prepared in manuscript.

Place	Date	Hour	Summary of Events and Information	Remarks and references to Appendices
HONDEGHEM	15-1-19		Captain H. HENDRIE took over command of Battalion owing absence of C.O. on leave	G.R.O.
	16-1-19		Battalion on fatigues	G.R.O.
			Usual routine of camp carried out	
	17-1-19		The Battalion Band colours presented to them on this day by the G.O.C. 59th Div.	G.R.O.
HONDEGHEM SIDING CAMP	18-1-19		Camp no longer functioning as Demob. camp. Nothing to report.	Reft
	19-1-19		Divine Service	Reft
	20-1-19		Nothing to record occurred.	Reft
	21-1-19		Nothing to record occurred	Reft
	22-1-19		Nothing to record occurred	Reft
	23-1-19		Nothing to record occurred	Reft
	24-1-19		Nothing to record occurred	Reft
	25-1-19		Nothing to record occurred. — Battalion warned will move shortly to DUNKIRK	Reft
	26-1-19		Nothing to record occurred. Divine Service	Reft
	27-1-19		Nothing to record occurred — Warned to move on 30th inst.	Reft
	28-1-19		Nothing to record occurred — Ration Strength 16 officers + 421 other ranks	P.S.S.
	29-1-19		Handed over Camp to 24th Bn Royal Welsh Fus.	P.S.S.
DUNKIRK	30-1-19		Entrained 09.00hrs at HONDEGHEM SIDING for DUNKIRK. Arrived DUNKIRK 15.00 hrs. Accommodated in "3" Huts.	Reft
"	31-1-19		Took over "B" CAMP from 11th Royal Scots Fus. and undertook Demob. Reception work.	Reft

M. Grehan Lt. Col.
28 B.R.F.

Army Form C. 2118.

WAR DIARY
or
INTELLIGENCE SUMMARY.
(Erase heading not required.)

Instructions regarding War Diaries and Intelligence Summaries are contained in F. S. Regs., Part II. and the Staff Manual respectively. Title pages will be prepared in manuscript.

Place	Date	Hour	Summary of Events and Information	Remarks and references to Appendices

Army Form C. 2118.

WAR DIARY
or
INTELLIGENCE SUMMARY.

(Erase heading not required.)

Original.

Confidential

WAR DIARY
February 1919
Volume XXII
26th Batt. Royal Welch Fus.

26TH BATTALION,
ROYAL WELCH
FUSILIERS.

Army Form C. 2118.

WAR DIARY
or
INTELLIGENCE SUMMARY.
(Erase heading not required.)

Instructions regarding War Diaries and Intelligence Summaries are contained in F. S. Regs., Part II. and the Staff Manual respectively. Title pages will be prepared in manuscript.

Place	Date	Hour	Summary of Events and Information	Remarks and references to Appendices
Dunkirk	1-2-19		Battalion employed in running "B" Camp & Demobilization Machinery - Dunkirk Area.	Regt.
"	2-2-19		No change	Regt.
"	3-2-19		No change	Regt.
"	4-2-19		No change	Regt.
"	5-2-19		No change	Regt.
"	6-2-19		No change	Regt.
"	7-2-19		No change. Staff of 6 Officers & 155 Other Ranks arrived ex 1/4" R.W.F. (Pioneers)	R.S.
"	8-2-19		Battalion took over No 5 Camp and relinquished "B" Camp.	R.S.
"	9-2-19		No change	Regt.
"	10-2-19		No change	Regt.
"	11-2-19		No change	Regt.
"	12-2-19		No change	Regt.
"	13-2-19		No change	Regt.
"	14-2-19		No change	Regt.
"	15-2-19		No change	Regt.
"	16-2-19		No change	Regt.

WAR DIARY
or
INTELLIGENCE SUMMARY.

(Erase heading not required.)

Army Form C. 2118.

Instructions regarding War Diaries and Intelligence Summaries are contained in F. S. Regs., Part II. and the Staff Manual respectively. Title pages will be prepared in manuscript.

Place	Date	Hour	Summary of Events and Information	Remarks and references to Appendices
Hursley	17-2-19		No change	[illeg]
"	18-2-19		No change. Two officers reported for duty ex 13th R.W.F. Three officers reported for duty ex 16th R.W.F.	[illeg]
"	19-2-19		No change	[illeg]
"	20-2-19		No change. Six officers reported for duty ex 2nd R.W.F. — Two officers reported ex 13th R.W.F. — Three officers reported ex 14th R.W.F. Four officers reported ex 17th R.W.F.	[illeg]
"	21-2-19		No change	[illeg]
"	22-2-19		No change. One officer & forty other ranks reported ex 13th R.W.F. — Two officers & 50 other ranks ex 14th R.W.F. — One officer & 50 other ranks ex 16th R.W.F.	[illeg]
"	23-2-19		No change	[illeg]
"	24-2-19		No change	[illeg]
"	25-2-19		No change	[illeg]
"	26-2-19		No change	[illeg]
"	27-2-19		No change	[illeg]
"	28-2-19		No change [illeg]	[illeg]

N.L. Gaskam
Lt Colonel
Cmdg. 20th (Reserve) Bn Royal Welsh Fus.

WAR DIARY
or
INTELLIGENCE SUMMARY.
(Erase heading not required.)

Army Form C. 2118.

Instructions regarding War Diaries and Intelligence Summaries are contained in F. S. Regs., Part II. and the Staff Manual respectively. Title pages will be prepared in manuscript.

Place	Date	Hour	Summary of Events and Information	Remarks and references to Appendices

A6945 Wt. W11422/M1160 350,000 12/16 D. D. & L. Forms/C./2118/14.

Army Form C. 2118.

WAR DIARY
or
INTELLIGENCE SUMMARY.

(Erase heading not required.)

Original.

WAR DIARY
March 1919
Volume XXXIV
26th Batt. Royal Welch Fus.

Confidential

WAR DIARY
or
INTELLIGENCE SUMMARY.
(Erase heading not required.)

Army Form C. 2118.

Place	Date	Hour	Summary of Events and Information	Remarks and references to Appendices
Dunkirk	1-3-19		Battalion relieved by 25th King's Liverpool Regt at No 5 Camp and returned to "B" Camp. Hospice for accommodation. Supplied 12 officers and 266 other ranks for local POW Coy detachments.	TRAS
	2-3-19		Lieut C.C. MARSTON MC & H.G. PARRY and 93 other ranks reported to 9th RWF.	RWS
	3-3-19		No change	RWS
	4-3-19		do	RWS
	5-3-19		do	RWS
	6-3-19		do	RWS
	7-3-19		do	RWS
	8-3-19		do	RWS
	9-3-19		do. Lieuts T.B. PRICE MC, W.D. RODERICK DSO MC, J.L. RALPH MC, 2/Lieuts M. THOMAS, F. THOMPSON DCM and E.S. SAUNDERS and 71 other ranks reported at 2nd, 14th, 16th RWF	TRAS
	10-3-19		No change	RWS
	11-3-19		do	RWS
	12-3-19		do. 8 other ranks to 9th RWF reported.	RWS
	13-3-19		do	RWS
	14-3-19			RWS

WAR DIARY
or
INTELLIGENCE SUMMARY.

Army Form C. 2118.

Place	Date	Hour	Summary of Events and Information	Remarks and references to Appendices
Dunkirk	15-3-19		Lieut O.T. JONES MC and 52 Other Ranks joined ex 17th R.W.F	Pers
	16-3-19		No change	Pers
	17-3-19		Lieut J.W. WATERS, 2nd Lieut W.J.E. PEPPER and 126 Other Ranks ex 1st Yorks & Lancashire Regt. joined	Pers
	18-3-19		No change	Pers
	19-3-19		A/Capt. H.W. TREGUNNA MC, Lieut W.M. BARBER, J. GOUGE, 2/Lieut W.J. DUNN, E.F. MESSE & H.G. WILLIAMS Capt. C.F. TISSINGTON MC, Lieut T. LLOYD, J. WATTS, 2/Lieut HODGSON and 129 Other Ranks joined battalion ex 15th Cheshire Regt.	Pers
			Proceeded on demobilisation	
	20-3-19		Other Ranks joined battalion ex 15th Cheshire Regt. Battalion moved camp and took over hutments on CHAMP DE MANOEUVRES, MALO-LES-BAINS from 2nd Batt. Cheshire Regt.	Pers
MALO-LES-BAINS	21-3-19		No change	Pers
	22-3-19		2nd Lieut T.G. ENGLISH and 8 Other Ranks joined ex 15th Cheshire Regt.	Pers
	23-3-19		9 Other Ranks ex 15th Cheshire Regt and 5 Other Ranks ex 9th R.W.F. joined. 2nd Lieut B. PYKETT proceeded U.K.	Pers
	24-3-19		6 Other Ranks ex Y&L R.W.F. and 2nd Lieut R.H. MORGAN & 2nd R.W.F. and 2/Lt E.T. WARREN NE YORK joined	Pers
	25-3-19		No change	Pers
	26-3-19		No change	Pers
			No change	Pers

Army Form C. 2118.

WAR DIARY
or
INTELLIGENCE SUMMARY.
(Erase heading not required.)

Instructions regarding War Diaries and Intelligence Summaries are contained in F. S. Regs., Part II. and the Staff Manual respectively. Title pages will be prepared in manuscript.

Place	Date	Hour	Summary of Events and Information	Remarks and references to Appendices
MARB. LES. BAINS	27-3-19		Officer Reinforcements – Lieut R.A. JONES of 16th R.W.F. and 2nd Lieut G.S. EDITH to 2nd R.W.F.	124.A
	28-3-19		No change. A/Capt M.M. CRIMMON, Lieut T.B. PRICE MC 2nd Lieut G.H. ANDERSON, Lieut ALEXANDER 2nd Lieut D.E. JAMES, M.X. LOWRIE proceeded for demobilization	124.B
	29-3-19		No change. 2nd Lieut R.S. THOMAS 3/Lieut IN DYE DEAN proceeded for demobilization	(Back)
	30-3-19		No change. Capt E.W. BRANT OC proceeded for demobilization	124.C
	31-3-19		No change.	124.D

W.L. Gardner
Lieut Colonel
Comg 26th Bn R.W.F.

A6945 Wt. W14422/M160 350,000 12/16 D. D. & L. Forms/C/2118/14

Army Form C. 2118.

WAR DIARY
or
INTELLIGENCE SUMMARY.

(Erase heading not required.)

Instructions regarding War Diaries and Intelligence Summaries are contained in F. S. Regs., Part II. and the Staff Manual respectively. Title pages will be prepared in manuscript.

Place	Date	Hour	Summary of Events and Information	Remarks and references to Appendices

A6945 Wt. W14422/M1160 350,000 12/16 D. D. & L. Forms/C./2118/14.

Army Form C. 2118.

WAR DIARY
or
INTELLIGENCE SUMMARY.

(Erase heading not required.)

No 10

Confidential

WAR DIARY

April 1919

Volume XXXV

26th R.W.Fus

Army Form C. 2118.

WAR DIARY
or
INTELLIGENCE SUMMARY.
(Erase heading not required.)

OF 26th ROYAL WELCH FUS
April 1st-30th.19.

Place	Date	Hour	Summary of Events and Information	Remarks and references to Appendices
MALO	1.4.19		Training Parade. Lt Roberts left Battn for leave to UK.	W.D.
"	2.4.19		Training Parade. No Change	W.D.
"	3.4.19		Parade. M.O. leave to UK. Capt Nolan 2/Lt V Copcock	W.D.
"	4.4.19		Training Parade. " " 2/Lt Caldwell 2/Lt Davies 2/Lt Jameson 217 Jameson 30 OR joined from 17th RWF. 2/Lt Goddard	W.D. Frog'l leave 2/Lt Goddard
"	5.4.19		C.O. Kit Inspection " " Lt Hayes 2/Lt Strickland 13 ORs joined from 9th RWF. 30 ORs from 15th RWF	W.D.
"	6.4.19 S		Divine Service	W.D.
"	7.4.19		Training Parade. Reinforcements. Lt W. Jones from 17th RWF. 3 OR from 1/6 RWF. 1 OR from 17th RWF	W.D.
"	8.4.19		Training Parade. Leave to UK. Lt Perry. Lt Hadlow 2/Lt Jossin.	W.D.
"	9.4.19		Training Parade. " " Lt C.C. Hargreaves (MO) Capt Dicas MC sun leave. 2/Lt B. Watson	W.D.
"	10.4.19		Training Parade. " " Lt Clayton	W.D.
"	11.4.19		Parade. MO. " 2/Lt Raper	W.D.
"	12.4.19		Training Parade. Rejoined from leave. 2/Lt Roper	W.D.
"	13.4.19 6		Div. Service. leave to UK. Capt. Birtwistle. 2/Lt Thompson (DCM)	W.D.
"	14.4.19		Div. Service. 5 OR joined from 1/6 RWF.	W.D.
"	15.4.19		Training Parade. 1/6 Change	W.D.
"	16.4.19		Training Parade. Route March. Rejoined from leave 2/Lt E. Jones.	W.D.
"	17.4.19 F		Training Parades " " 2/Lt R.H.L. Morgan.	W.D.
"	18.4.19 F		Parade. M.O. Exchange Capt Phillipson & Catlow for Change to Florence	W.D.
"	19.4.19 F		Parade. Services from leave 2/Lt Wicker. 2/Lt Copless	W.D.
"	20.4.19 S		Corps Off Kit Inspection " " 2/Lt W. Jeffries	W.D.
"	21.4.19		Div. Service " " 2/Lt Calauta	W.D.
"	22.4.19		Parade. G/C. Lt Lloyd proceeds to UK to arty in Russia. From leave 2/Lt Stoddart.	W.D.
"	23.4.19		Training Parades. " " Lt Hayes " " Lt Hulme Lt Brook Lt Revens 2/Lt Roberts. Lt Perry 2/Lt Jossin 2/Lt Jameson	cm
"	24.4.19 S		Training Parades 2/Lt Wynne. Transfer to SWB Punch from leave Lt Hulme Lt Brook Lt Revens (C.Lt Leggatt sujance)	W.D.
"	25.4.19 F		Parade. M.O.	W.D.
"	26.4.19		Training Parade. From leave Capt Vincent. Lt G.E. Evans	W.D.
"	27.4.19 S		Brit. Ceremony 2/Lt Jameson 2/Lt Kelly (commissioned)	W.D.
"	28.4.19		Divine Service Lt Watts leave to UK. From leave Capt Boston 2/Lt Thompson 2/Lt Clarke 2/Lt Cox	cm
"	29.4.19		Training Parade. All Regt Transport Leaves from 48 ORs joined from 2nd and 17th RWF	W.D.
"	30.4.19		Training Parade 129 ORs joined from S.W.B. 8 off. 213 ORs formed 1st Bn army systems	W.D.
"			Training Parade) 2/Lt Saunders from leave. to Battn Regiments in Egypt. N. Garters x in Eng conch. 26th R.W.F.	

Army Form C. 2118.

WAR DIARY
or
INTELLIGENCE SUMMARY.

(Erase heading not required.)

Instructions regarding War Diaries and Intelligence Summaries are contained in F. S. Regs., Part II and the Staff Manual respectively. Title pages will be prepared in manuscript.

Place	Date	Hour	Summary of Events and Information	Remarks and references to Appendices

A5834 Wt.W4973/M687 730,000 8/16 D. D. & L. Ltd. Forms/C.2118/13.

www.ingramcontent.com/pod-product-compliance
Lightning Source LLC
Chambersburg PA
CBHW081440160426
43193CB00013B/2341